*I*NTERIM *M*ANAGEMENT

INTERIM MANAGEMENT

A New Dimension in Corporate Performance

GODFREY GOLZEN

EXECUTIVE INTERIM MANAGEMENT
EGON ZEHNDER INTERNATIONAL / BOER & CROON / EUROVENTURES

———————————— E I M ————————————

KOGAN
PAGE

Disclaimer

Where the masculine pronoun has been used it stems from a desire to avoid ugly and cumbersome language, and no discrimination, prejudice or bias is intended.

First published in 1992
Reprinted 1993

Kogan Page Limited
120 Pentonville Road
London N1 9JN

© Executive Interim Management

British Library Cataloguing in Publication Data

A CIP record for this book is available from the British Library.

ISBN 0 7494 0363 2

Typeset by DP Photosetting, Aylesbury, Bucks
Printed in England by Clays Ltd, St Ives plc

Contents

6   Why Not Go It Alone? — Interim Management Versus Independent Consultancy   87

7   Effecting the Introduction: Client Company and Interim Manager   99

Foreword

As pressures continue to grow to maintain profits and growth and to contain business costs, so companies face an ever greater challenge in reinforcing or replacing that single most valuable resource — high performance management.

Required are total professionals; managers with that combination of vision, experience and sheer determination that delivers commercial success. As specialists or generalists, such executives must be able to function in national or international markets, in industrialised or less advanced economies and with sophisticated or relatively primitive facilities.

Interim management is developing at speed because it precisely responds to these needs. It is now clear that it is often the interim manager, results driven and free from corporate conventions, rather than the permanent representative who is best equipped to deliver imaginative, cost-effective solutions whether in acquisitions, joint ventures, disposals, new market development, productivity improvement or crisis management.

Interim management is among the more significant new

dimensions to emerge in the quest for strong corporate performance. That the use of interim managers will continue to grow is evident. Companies that use them will stand to achieve appreciable competitive advantage.

Cees H Boer
Founding Partner
Boer & Croon Management Consultants BV

Acknowledgements

Special thanks are due to Executive Interim Management worldwide who initiated this timely book and to numerous interim managers and interim management companies mentioned and quoted in the text, all of whom took time to give the author invaluable information on the subject. Their help is gratefully acknowledged. Thanks are due to Robert Barrow for permission to reproduce the ATIES Professional Indemnity Plan.

ABOUT EXECUTIVE INTERIM MANAGEMENT

Executive Interim Management originated in Holland in 1978. Since then it has expanded across Europe and into Australasia, managing change or transition through its team of interim managers. Executive Interim Management normally executes the chief executive or finance director roles but does undertake other 'director' roles.

Organisations use interim managers for various reasons; an unexpected vacancy at a high level due to illness or departure, or crisis management and control, or turnarounds.

Since being founded, Executive Interim Management has handled over 1000 assignments for banks, insurance, transport, manufacturing, engineering and service companies, non-profit organisations and local and national governments. All client details remain confidential.

ABOUT THE AUTHOR

Godrey Golzen is a visiting fellow at Cranfield School of Management and a specialist writer on business and employment. He is a well-known contributor to the national press and author of many best-selling books including *Going Freelance*, *Taking Up a Franchise*, *Working Abroad* and *Working for Yourself*. He is also editor of *Human Resources* magazine.

1

Doing Business in an Age of Uncertainty

Every decade or so, a business book appears which somehow encapsulates everything that is in the air at the time. Back in the seventies, it was E F Schumacher's *Small Is Beautiful.*[1] Apart from being the forerunner of many of today's concerns about the relationship between environmental issues and business strategy, it challenged the 1960s idea that very large organisations produce economies of scale and create a synthesis which enables the parts to draw on the strength of the whole. It showed that instead they spawned immense and unwieldy bureaucracies that simply could not respond to the sort of business problems that need a quick response; and furthermore that the people in them lost all sense of belonging to something they could identify with.

At the beginning of the 1980s, Tom Peters and Bob Waterman wrote *In Search of Excellence*[2] which argued that what they called 'the rational model' of the organisation, with its over-zealous centralised planning, its focus on systems, hierarchies and procedures, stifled initiative and motivation among the people who work for it. Anticipating the notion of 'empowerment' of people at all levels of the organisation, instead of a command and control system which lays down from the top detailed plans for everyone to follow, they wrote that 'we see excellent companies dividing things up and pushing authority down the line.'

Peters followed that up towards the end of the 1980s with another influential book *Thriving On Chaos*[3]. Here he looked at what had become the dominant theme of the decade — change — and suggested that the utmost flexibility in ideas and procedures was the only way in which organisations could cope with the environment being changed almost daily by rapid technological advancement.

Arguably, the book of the 1990s has been Professor Charles Handy's *The Age of Unreason*[4] which takes the ideas of Schumacher and Peters a stage further and closer to the theme of interim management. A more appropriate title might have been 'The Age of Uncertainty', because that has been the dominant theme of the world economy since the stock market crash of October 1987.

> **Using interim managers and specialists, rather than making permanent additions to the payroll, makes good sense in times of economic uncertainty or when, for other reasons, the way ahead is not clear.**

During this time we have seen the fall, throughout the world, of many of the companies which were most admired in the eighties. We have also seen changes in political systems, and hence of market opportunities, that had been unthinkable before they actually happened — about as unthinkable, in fact, as that companies like Bond and Fairfax in Australia, Campeau and Trump in the USA, Nixdorf in Germany, Phillips in the Netherlands and Saatchi & Saatchi in the UK, among others, should be in varying states of disarray by the nineties.

In a sense Handy's book sets out the justification for interim management, as well as suggesting indirectly where this concept fits into the future of organisations. His argument is that in an age of change and turmoil, organisations will have to travel light if they are going to be able to adapt quickly enough to survive. In practice this means that they are going to have to expand and contract their workforce according to demand. Permanent employees might consist of a fairly small central core working in functions that cannot be contracted out — for instance that of actually managing and administering the much larger flexible workforce of contractors, consultants, freelancers, interim managers and part-timers. Recent research confirms this view. A report entitled 'The Future of Offices' by the Business Design Group and the forecasting company, Henley Centre Ireland, is based on the premise that

> the organisation of the future will make far more conscious and widespread use of sub-contracting as a means of matching output activity to demand levels[5]

When one reads in *Fortune* magazine[6] that of Heinz's 50,000 employees world-wide only 150 are now based at the corporate headquarters, it shows how far along that road we have already travelled. True, Heinz's 49,850 or so other people are still employees, but how much longer will they all be so?

An increasing number of commentators now point to the future creation of what one might call a 'just in time workforce' to match the 'just in time' techniques of industrial production. The principle is that instead of stockpiling materials and components, firms should merely have enough of them on hand to fulfil orders in the short term.

INTERIM MANAGEMENT: ROLES AND DEFINITION

Flexible manning is certainly one of the contexts in which interim management can be deployed, though up to now it has been brought in largely as a reaction to change and crisis, rather than as a way of anticipating it. That may be one of the developments to come. Another may be that interim managers will become a regular part of the transient 'leaves' of what Charles Handy calls 'the shamrock organisation'. But if we look at the here and now, the roles in which interim managers are appearing, and which will be discussed in this book, are:

- Bridging gaps, pending a regular appointment, or filling in while a search is going on[7]

- Managing a crisis, following a dismissal, death or unexpected departure. Providing first aid in the event of the withdrawal of bank support or the threatened loss of a key customer

- Managing a turnaround, often one too risky to attract a permanent candidate. Taking charge of an organisation in deep trouble, in what has often been termed a 'company doctor' role

- Holding the fort, when a board is not clear what sort of person to appoint to a senior job and would rather make an interim appointment until its outlines become clear

- Management of a change of culture, strategy, policy or corporate structure, especially when there is a need for urgent action to offset an external threat, such as a potential hostile bid

- Taking charge of a specific project, such as a factory or office move; or the speculative entry of a company into a new market or product area

- Part-time management when circumstances do not warrant a full-time role

- Stepping in to stabilise the situation following a merger or acquisition

- Putting a company or business unit into a fit state prior to a sell-off

- Strengthening the management team on an interim basis, following a management buy-out or buy-in

- Applying special expertise or know-how to a project out of line with a company's normal business activities.

All these various eventualities have been summed up in a doctoral thesis produced in the Netherlands by Irene Schoemakers on the activities of Executive Interim Management (EIM). Her words could well serve as a definition of interim management when she writes that:

> 'Interim management is the temporary placement of highly qualified managers with the specific task of ensuring continuity within an organisation. It can also be put in place to augment the skills of an existing management team.'[8]

INTERIM MANAGEMENT AND NEW CAREER PATTERNS

When I first wrote about this concept in The *Sunday Times* in 1988, it produced a phenomenal response. The interim management firms I mentioned had literally thousands of enquiries from managers interested in the idea. Some, inevitably, were from people on the job market, but a very high proportion came from those well established in their careers; several of them were main board directors of nationally known companies. So why would people want to exchange security for the hazards of freelance self-employment?

One answer to that question is: *what* security? The American management guru Rosabeth Moss Kanter expresses a widely held view when she writes that 'beliefs in the large corporation and the safety of a corporate career are rapidly disappearing.'[9] One of the principal effects of the age of uncertainty is that we have all seen (or personally experienced) careers abruptly terminated, increasingly by circumstances outside the control of those affected.

[17]

> **Interim management is a concept which meets both individual aspirations for autonomy and the needs of organisations who want to 'travel light' in order to react quickly to a rapidly changing environment.**

This is not a trend tied to economic cycles. It reflects a situation where companies are at the mercy of global competition and of challenges that can come out of nowhere. In order to survive they have to undergo chameleon-like changes, such as that of Grand Metropolitan which, in the course of a decade, changed from a property company to a hotel group and then into a food and drink conglomerate. Firms are both trying new things ('ready, fire, aim', as Tom Peters puts it) and sticking to the knitting. Sometimes, as in the case of the Prudential's disastrous excursion into estate agency, they return to the knitting much chastened. They are both trying to run lean and build up muscle in attempting to go global in their activities. They are under desperate pressure from financial institutions to grow, but support is quickly withdrawn if they stumble. Boards may say that people are their most important asset, and genuinely believe it, but the money men are very unsentimental about people if the asset fails to produce a quick return.

It is a terribly unstable environment in which to build a business and to take on permanent people, except for the diminishing number of tasks and functions for which there is demonstrable long-term demand. But it is also an unstable environment in which to build a career and the people who mostly lose out are the older echelons, the over forties. As a result managers are changing their thinking from loyalty to commitment. Their loyalty is to themselves and to their families. Their commitment is to the task. That is a characteristic of many interim managers, as is their age and career pattern. They are mostly senior managers over 40 who have kept their eye on the ball and seen which way the play is going.

Another characteristic is the change of attitude arising out of the growth of the enterprise culture. Many managers who have reached middle age are now tempted by the desire to strike out for themselves and increasingly they have the financial resources to do so. Real incomes have risen sharply over the last 20 years. It is no longer entirely true to say that you cannot make money working for someone else. Stock options, the rise in the value of house prices and lower marginal tax rates have made a lot of people modestly wealthy. At forty-something they will probably have paid off their mortgage and their children may well have completed their education. That is the time, they feel, to change direction and to work for themselves. Managers who think along these lines also make some of the best interim managers.

In addition, there is a further aspect of changing attitudes to work. With a more highly skilled workforce — the members of the 'knowledge organisation', the coming into being of which was forecast by Peter Drucker over 20 years ago — comes a keener sense of autonomy. It has been cleverly seized on by the employment agency Reed in its advertisements for fREEDom as being one of the attractions of temporary secretarial work. In fact this kind of work has undergone a complete change of status in the past decade. 'Temps' used to be a rather lowly regarded species, used to fill in during holidays or absences, or on drudgery tasks that permanent secretary/typists could not be asked to tackle. Now temporary secretaries are often highly qualified, highly paid people who prefer the autonomy of working for themselves and the variety of doing so in different settings. The fact that an increasing number of recruitment firms are now providing an interim management service is a sign that they consider it probable that this trend will move upmarket.

A HIGH QUALITY RESOURCE

The kind of people who become interim managers represent a high quality human resource. They combine an entrepreneurial spirit with wisdom and experience. As companies have cut out layers of management and created more headroom for young high fliers they have become increasingly conscious of the fact that they have lost much of their collective wisdom: the contacts, the experience, the collective know-how. It is these qualities that make interim managers such an effective resource. One of the points made about them is that they can step into any situation and be more or less immediately effective. They do not have to traverse the long learning curve of their younger colleagues — but they still have the energy of people in their peak years. Many, in fact, represent a kind of 'lost generation' of management. As Anne Ferguson has put it in an article in *The Independent On Sunday*:

> Some companies are cutting middle managers they will need in future. Others will find that they have excised their next generation of managers[10]

> Managers who have chosen a new career as interims have a rare mix of experience, wisdom and entrepreneurial spirit. The fact that they are often over-qualified for the tasks they undertake makes them more, not less, well-equipped to carry them out.

One firm has recognised this and created their own group of interim managers. Faced with the problem of thinning out a highly skilled workforce of which some 8 per cent were over 50, IBM (UK) has formed a separate company, called *Skillbase*. Rather than putting its older executives into early retirement — and therefore losing the skills in which it has invested years of training — it offers them the chance to go on working for the company in an interim role. They are guaranteed 90 days work a year with IBM for two years. A condition of the scheme is that they have to be available for work for nine months of the year but they can choose the three months in which they do not want to work.

Skillbase is a valuable service, not only internally when some special expertise is called for, but also to IBM clients who need high level consultancy advice from time to time. But it has attracted attention from other companies as well. 'We negotiate rates with them on a basis similar to executive leasing', says Skillbase's managing director. 'It will have a very similar set of advantages for them, inasmuch as that they will be able to take on skilled staff flexibly, in response to specific projects or work fluctuations, rather than building up the payroll.'

A further advantage is that, as with interim managers in general, Skillbase members are very flexible with regard to working hours. A lot of computer operations depend on round-the-clock working. Older executives have been found to be more ready to take on assignments calling for unsocial hours than younger ones with family responsibilities.

Not many companies in the course of downsizing their payroll are able to offer interim management assignments to the people involved on the scale of IBM, but they might be well advised to hold on to their services on a periodic basis by offering them some guaranteed work. That guarantee could then be used as a basis for putting them in touch with an interim management organisation, who could explore further possibilities for part-time or short term assignments.

A STORY OF MARKET GROWTH

Although there are no precise figures for the size of the UK market for interim managers, its annual fee value has been estimated at £25m–£30m. That figure is comparable with the USA, where a recent report in *Consultants News* gives an estimate of $50m–$75. However, the total figure for independent consultants, essentially carrying out interim management-related assignments, is reckoned to be much larger — perhaps three or four times the size of the formal interim management market. For instance in the USA, it is thought there are some 200,000 active independent management consultants who take on interim work. The report describes what it calls 'executive temporaries' as 'the fastest growing segment of the burgeoning multi-billion-dollar temporary market'.

But acceptance of the formal interim management concept, it is fair to say, has so far been greater on the continent of Europe. For instance, EIM (Executive Interim Management), started in Holland 13 years ago, where it operated under the brand name of BCG Interim Management. In 1990 their turnover in Holland was £8 million, and EIM is now experiencing rapid growth in Belgium, France and Germany.[11]

> **The status of the growing number of firms getting into interim management is a sure sign that those best equipped to recognise trends have spotted it as an idea whose time has come.**

In the UK, the expectation is that interim management will grow by about 20 per cent a year. Both the number and status of the firms getting into it is significant. Typically they include offshoots of well-known firms in executive search and management consultancy, such as EIM (51 per cent owned by Europe's leading executive search company, Egon Zehnder), Protem (set up by Heidrick & Struggles) and the PA Consulting Group. Some of the firms involved have set up a co-ordinating body, The Association of Temporary & Interim Executive Services. They include:

- P-E Inbucon (which in this context is associated with the Confederation of British Industry)

- Albemarle Interim Management Services, a subsidiary of a well-known search and selection consultancy

- GMS Consultancy Ltd, essentially a specialist firm in executive leasing

- Ernst & Young Temporary Executive Service, an offshoot

of a leading firm of accountants and management consultants

- Barton Interim Management, which grew out of a West of England executive search firm and remains primarily to serve the needs of that region. Varley Walker Interim Management Ltd also has a mainly regional base — in this case the West Midlands and the north of England.

On the European Continent, EIM, including its Dutch associate BCG, is the market leader, with 8 European offices (though it faces competition from two Swiss firms, Adia and Brainforce) and two in Australia. In the USA about 30 firms are involved in interim management, most of them established since 1987. They are apparently growing very rapidly. For instance, one firm, Interim Management Corp, is reported to have seen revenues rise to $1m within two years of starting operations.

THE ROLES OF INTERIM MANAGEMENT FIRMS

As the market grows, it is becoming apparent that firms are developing and operating in different ways, though there are similarities in basic practice — points that will be explored more fully later. EIM, for instance, is seen as a top of the range player, filling positions at the level of chief executive and senior functional executive. It takes full responsibility for the work performed by its interims and keeps in close weekly contact with them during the course of the job. 'We are marketing a service, not bodies', says its managing partner, Robert Mark.

Other firms, such as GMS, take a more employment agency-related approach. The latter specifically say, for instance: 'We are an agency and do not take responsibility for the work done.' They add, however, that 'we keep in touch with the client and the executive to ensure that the assignment is proving satisfactory to both sides.' To a greater or lesser degree of formality, this is common practice among reputable interim management firms — more so than among employment agencies proper. In general these consider their job done once the client has selected a candidate.

The main emphasis on ensuring a satisfactory outcome for interim management assignments is, however, based on careful selection of the interim executives themselves. This is not just a question of providing a fit between the assignment, the individual and the client organisation. Another distinction between interim management firms and employment agencies is that the former aim not only to provide a match between the person and the task, when one comes up; they also rigorously select the interim managers who go on their databank in the first instance.

The rigorous selection methods applied by intermediaries to those who want to become interim managers provides quality assurance for clients.

The way interim management operates is that interim management companies maintain a pool of potential candidates for such assignments, organised according to industry knowledge, functional skills, qualifications, experience, age and so forth. But they receive many more enquiries from individuals who want to work as interim managers than are ever accepted for enrolment into the pool or on to the database. In Chapter 4 we will deal in more detail with selection criteria, but suffice it to say here that only about 10 per cent are considered suitable material. Some firms work in an even more rigorous fashion, and vet candidates down to a small, selective pool. For example, EIM invites managers to join the pool only after extensive vetting. Their aim is to build up a stable pool of managers they can use over and over again. They do not hold a databank.

It is the application of these rigorous selection criteria — as rigorous as those applied by executive search firms in compiling a short-list for a permanent job — which, from the client's point of view, makes working through an established interim management firm a better course of action than relying on informal methods, such as the old boy network. Interim management firms also claim that because of the size and quality of their database they can actually offer clients a wider and deeper pool of both generalists and specialists to choose from than management consultants can put forward.

Management consultancies are often the chief competitors of interim management firms when it comes to handling temporary assignments. It is interesting to note, however, that the Dutch observer of the UK interim management scene previously quoted cited the preference of UK executives for relying on the old boy network to fill senior posts on a temporary basis as one of the reasons why formal approaches to interim management through a recognised intermediary have been slow to take off in the UK. It is reasonable to assume that just as executive search has largely taken over from the old boy network in making permanent appointments, working through an interim management firm will, in the future, be seen to be superior to this more casual, if time-honoured, way of sourcing temporary executives.

INTERIM MANAGEMENT: THE INDIVIDUAL PERSPECTIVE

There is one big difference between interim management firms and executive search firms; and one big similarity between the former and employment agencies. Interim management firms take a percentage of what the client pays for the services of the interim manager to cover their own overheads and profit.

As a broad rule of thumb, firms providing interim managers take about 30 per cent of the fee income for this purpose. Those who work with an interim management firm find that the costs are justified by the following factors:

[25]

- The credibility of working through a recognised company who can point to rigorous selection criteria and a track record of having successfully completed previous interim management assignments and project management.

- Ongoing involvement of the interim management company and, in some cases, accountability.

- Negotiation of fees and terms in what are often grey areas for a stand-alone individual.

- A formal or informal network of fellow interim managers.

A final point worth making is that the rigorous selection process that takes place is itself a way for the individual of knowing whether he has what it takes to follow a demanding, though satisfying, new career track.

EXECUTIVE SUMMARY

To adapt in a rapidly-changing economy and environment, organisations are going to have to expand and contract their workforce according to demand, and there will be more widespread use of contracting out work.

Interim management offers specialised, high-level, 'temporary' assistance to a company, without increasing the liabilities/commitments entailed in employment permanent staff.

Interim management also meets individual aspirations for autonomy and appeals to the successful, experienced professional with entrepreneurial spirit.

The concept of interim management has been embraced principally by the US and continental Europe, particularly Belgium and Germany. It is expected that it will grow in the UK by 20 per cent per annum.

A number of the major firms involved in executive leasing in the UK have set up a co-ordinating body, The Association of Temporary and Interim Executive Services. Rigorous selection methods are applied by the intermediaries to guarantee quality assurance to clients.

The benefits offered to an interim manager by an intermediary are credibility, fee and terms negotiation, marketing, client and fellow interim manager contact.

REFERENCES

1. Schumacher, E F (1974) *Small Is Beautiful*, Sphere, London.
2. Peters, T J and Waterman, R H (1972) *In Search of Excellence*, Harper & Row, New York.

[27]

3. Peters, Tom (1988) *Thriving on Chaos*, Pan Books, London.

4. Handy, Charles (1989) *The Age of Unreason*, Hutchinson, London.

5. The Future Of Offices, (1991) Business Design Group, Bristol.

6. Stewart, T A, A User's Guide To Power, *Fortune*, 6 November 1989.

7. A number of interim management providers in the UK have close links with search firms. To name just some of them: EIM (Egon Zehnder), Stream Resources (Spencer Stuart), Albemarle Interim Management Services (The Albemarle Group), PA Executive Leasing (PA Consulting Group), Varley-Walker Interim Management Ltd (with Varley-Walker & Partners).

8. Executive Interim Management: Het bedrijf en die managers in relatie tot de Engelse cultuur, economieen sociale factoren, Rijksuniversiteit te Leiden, 1989.

9. Kanter, R M (1989) *When Giants Learn To Dance*, Simon & Schuster, New York.

10. How Executives Manage The Dole, *The Independent On Sunday*, 3 June 1991.

11. The links in the structure of Executive Interim Management (EIM) are interesting because they illustrate the various kinds of parties that are getting involved in interim management. EIM is 51 per cent owned by the search firm Egon Zehnder, in partnership with a venture capital firm, Euroventures and a Dutch management consultancy, Boer & Croon. The two latter firms are also the joint owners of BCG Holdings, which owns BCG Interim Management.

2

Interim Management In Action

A *Sunday Times* article written by Terry Lunn, personnel director at Joshua Tetley, recently described interim management as 'a powerful alternative to conventional recruitment and resourcing practices.' To some extent, as indicated in the previous chapter, its power lies in the validity of the idea of 'just in time' management in situations of economic or corporate uncertainty. But it also derives its strength from the calibre of the kind of people who are choosing to become interim managers.[1]

There are two main problems about gaining recognition of this fact from potential clients. One is that articles about interim management have termed it 'executive temping' or leasing. A number of intermediaries, such as P–E International and Ernst & Young, do in fact describe their service as being the provision of temporary executives. That is probably why the Association of Temporary and Interim Managers has adopted the word in its title, but it can be subject to misunderstanding, because 'temping' is connected in the minds of many companies with rather low level tasks.[2] How, they ask, can a 'temp' address an important functional or general management issue?

In reality the similarity of interim management with 'office temping' goes no further than the fact that assignments are not permanent and the client can terminate it at any time, at short notice. Beyond that, there is a world of difference between interim managers and what they do, and notions associated with office temping.

WHO ARE THE INTERIM MANAGERS?

The other doubt that many firms have about interim management and which they express more or less openly is this: who are these interim managers? What is their background and qualifications? The suspicion, unstated or otherwise, is that they are redundant executives filling in time between jobs: what one interim management firm condemns as the 'buddy, can you spare a job' syndrome.

Interim management is a career in itself — it is not a way of filling in time between jobs. Interim management is one of the ways in which independent consultants operate.

In fact most interim management companies would agree with the view that

> It is not work for filling in between permanent jobs. It is a career in itself, and requires a project-oriented, time conscious approach.

Otherwise the danger is that they will not be 100 per cent focused on the task in hand. They might even leave it if a permanent job offer comes up, as actually happened in cases in the past. Some will, it is certainly true, have been made redundant, but that's simply a fact of life. A sure sign that this occurs is that executive search companies, who used to shun outplacement consultants, now call them regularly to see if they have anyone on their books who might be the answer to a search problem.[3]

However, quite a large number of senior people who have experienced redundancy have no desire to get back into permanent full-time employment — or they may have hit the age barrier (50/55 +). One of the problems that firms have is that though they acknowledge the ability of older managers to bring balance and wisdom to the management of change, they may only need it in relation to specific situations or projects for a given period of time. Too many older managers on the payroll block the paths of promotion for young high-fliers. Yet the latter lack the hard-to-define, accumulated know-how that comes with time and experience and which enables them to tackle a new task from day one. Interim management, by definition, solves this dilemma; so it is in these circumstances, among others, that the concept comes into its own because it dovetails both corporate objectives and individual second career aims.

Ahoy for a turnaround

One man who epitomises this is Jaap Mortier, the interim chief executive of Ahoy, a 24,000 square metre, multi-million Guilder turnover conference, exhibition, sports and leisure complex on the edge of Rotterdam. His experiences there also shows why these qualities are needed.

Mortier already had a formidable and varied senior management record with a number of multinationals — latterly as a member of the main board of Douwe Egbert, the Dutch subsidiary of the American food conglomerate Sarah Lee — before retiring in 1984. Though financially comfortable, after a year or two he was attracted back into interim management

[31]

by BCG, the market leaders in Holland, itself also an area where interim management has taken a firmer hold than in any other European country.

In April 1988 BCG presented him with a challenge so tough that he found it irresistible. Ahoy had been owned by the municipality of Rotterdam and despite its high profile — among its facilities, is a 10,000 seater Sports Palace which is one of the indoor venues for WCT tennis tournaments — it was making crippling losses. 'We were asked in the first instance to prepare a business plan which would enable the shareholders to make a decision about whether or not to keep it going', he recalls. 'We found one of the problems was that the buildings and facilities were in very poor shape. The whole place had been run in a typical public sector way, more or less divorced from what the market was looking for. But it was too dilapidated to compete in a more commercial environment.'

Mortier and his team sized up what needed to be done within a couple of weeks — he says that a good interim manager should be able to do that, even in a rather complex situation. 'You have to ask whether there is a cure and what it is. It generally boils down to seeing what the company can do well and building up the activities concerned with that.'

As a result of that process, he then put forward a proposal which would have meant an investment of 25 million Guilders. 'The shareholders liked the plan — but they told us they had no money.' At that BCG resigned, but were asked to stay on and to do the best they could with existing resources.

What followed was a tough turnaround process, combining staff cuts, the elimination of loss-making events and price increases for those that were identified as being commercially viable. In April 1989, Mortier came forward with a new financial plan and on the evidence he had by this time produced that Ahoy could be saved, it was accepted. 'We were able to forecast a profit for the next financial year of 5–6 million Guilders. On that basis the next stage of my assignment was to put the new plan in place and train my successor.'

When I spoke to Mortier at the end of 1990, he was

preparing for his departure in January 1991. Though Ahoy was clearly back on its feet and humming with business, there was still a lot to be done. Did he not want to stay and see it through further? 'A good interim manager mustn't get too involved,' he replied. 'If you do, it makes things too difficult for your successor. Eighteen to twenty-four months is about the maximum length of time to stay in an interim assignment.'

He also said that though he had been well rewarded for what was clearly a notable achievement in turning Ahoy round, he had no regrets about not having had a financial stake in the recovery operation. Interim managers, he is convinced, should be rewarded with high fees, rather than with equity. 'It's not a good idea for an interim to have a financial interest in the outcome of his activities. The temptation may be to maximise short-term returns at the expense of long-term strategy. For instance we're on a very valuable site here. We could have sold out at any time for 80 million Guilders. But that wouldn't have been in the long-term interests of the shareholders — or the community.'

The example of Ahoy illustrates what is meant by interim management combining short-term action with a long-term view. Jaap Mortier also says that, experienced manager though he is, he owed a considerable debt to BCG. 'The briefing of what the job entailed was vital. And there's always someone there that you can talk to if something isn't going according to plan — either another interim manager with functional expertise or one of BCG's staff who can mediate with the client.'

PERSONAL GOALS AND SOCIAL TRENDS

There are, however, many other reasons why people become interim managers. One that research has shown is increasingly coming to the fore is that a larger proportion of 'fortyish' high fliers are 'actively thinking about quitting the boardroom.'[4] to devote more time to personal goals. These include setting up as independent consultants.

Another factor is that age levels for full-time, all-the-year-round work are tending to fall. Already the future envisaged by Charles Handy is happening. He believes that by the year 2000 full-time jobs will take no more than 25 years of a working life, as compared to the current 40–45 years. 'Work won't stop for people after 50', he writes in *The Age of Unreason*, 'but it won't be the same sort of work; it will not be a job as they have known it.'

> **Interim management is part of a new emerging pattern of work, in which people will be in salaried employment for only part of their working lives.**

Interim management is a strong claimant for this new role of what Handy calls 'third age careers' and what the Americans are calling 'new age careers'. There are a lot of able managers out there who have retired in their early fifties but who still have plenty of energy left, as well as twenty-plus years of line management experience. There is also an increasing number of people in their late thirties and early forties who have turned their backs on the corporate rat race.[5] They can be a godsend to companies who need a strong, experienced hand on the tiller to bring things back on course.

Right second time

Tom Peters is not an apostle of 'right first time'. Though he has abandoned many of the doctrines put forward in his best-seller *In Search of Excellence*, one he does stick to is 'try it, fix it, do it again'. What, he asks, would have happened to aviation if the 'right first time' brigade had rejected the hedge-hopping prototypes of the early days of flying?

The necessity to take action first and get it right later is one that particularly affects companies that are trying to expand across borders. Working in literally unfamiliar territory increases the risks. Thus Autronica, Norways's leaders in fire alarm systems, picked the wrong person to head up their push into the UK market and turned to Executive Interim Management to get them out of deep trouble.

The man EIM sent in was typical of the kind of managers who turn to interim management as a career. Merlin Alty is in his early fifties, an engineer with an accountancy qualification, and a wealth of senior line management experience as well as technical expertise. When his last job as chief executive of the electronics subsidiary of an major engineering group disappeared in the course of company reorganisation, he decided to go out on his own. 'I'd become aware of the fact that there are a lot of small, engineering-based companies run by technocrats who are short of management skills', he says. 'They're funded by venture capital firms who often don't really understand the business they're investing in, and therefore have no idea about what to do when things go wrong. I thought there was a niche there for someone with my kind of background to advise them.'

He was right about that and landed a number of interesting interim management assignments — for instance sorting out a management buy-out that had gone wrong — but he found he was spending too much time marketing his services in order to maintain continuity of work. He read about EIM in *The Sunday Times*. 'The connection with Egon Zehnder and Euroventures gives them a lot of credibility in the market', he says. However he stresses that he remains an independent operator. 'I have no sole contractual relationship with them, except in relation to particular assignments. I am free to undertake work on my own or even to work with other interim management firms.'

Having worked in a number of interim managers' roles, Alty has found some common themes running through his experiences. 'You've got to act as an executive, not as a consultant. You've got to be tough, but tactful. You're an agent of change but it's easier for an interim manager to take that role than someone coming from the inside, who is burdened with history. It's the ideal preliminary to handing over to a permanent appointee.'

Alty admits that it is not an easy message to put across to companies. 'They say "our business is too complicated to hand over to an interim" but most problems are generic. They're either financial, organisational or to do with people. What business the company is in isn't vital in tackling such problems, though it does help to have an interim manager with relevant experience.'

A profile of one kind of interim manager is the early retired who after a few months of what they thought was going to be the good life, find they actually need the stimulus of work; not a job in the conventional sense but an active working involvement for some part of the year or some days a week. They are an enormous and under-used human resource, especially for smaller and medium-sized companies, who need specific skills but cannot afford them full-time; or in situations where specialist expertise is needed over a short period*.

The tough road to privatisation

Interim management is often described as 'the management of change'. No process epitomises this concept more strongly

---

* Throughout this text I shall be using masculine personal pronouns in referring to interim managers. This usage is in its unisex sense, but in fact there are as yet very few female applicants for interim management jobs. The reason is that interim management firms look in the main for people over 45. There are as yet very few female managers in that age group who have the right qualifications. But this is merely a matter of time.

[36]

than the privatisation of public sector bodies, which has been going on throughout both western and eastern Europe since the late 1980s.

Public sector privatisation involves profound changes of both a technical and cultural nature. Severn Trent Water, the second largest water authority in the UK, was therefore in an awkward position when, with the advent of privatisation, no suitable person had been found to take over the key role of company secretary. Severn Trent was aware that it would have to meet a whole range of statutory requirements imposed by the Companies Act, as well as coping with the cultural changes that would come with being answerable to shareholders, rather than civil servants.

To cope with the workload and hold the fort until it could make a permanent appointment, the Authority got in touch with Albemarle Interim Management Services (AIMS). It came up with Neil Skinner, formerly Assistant Company Secretary with Allied Lyons. 'For between three and four days a week, Neil Skinner helped to re-shape the Authority into a public company', writes AIMS' managing director John Hird. 'Privatisation meant the formation of over a dozen subsidiaries, and the appointment of boards of directors for each of them.' In addition pension funds and employee share schemes had to be set up and all the mechanics for share registration had to be put in place.

Neil Skinner's immense experience meant, however, that he could handle it all by coming in three or four days a week. After the flotation was completed, he remained in an advisory capacity to oversee some of the technical details. The final part of his assignment was to prepare the ground for a successor: a classical way of progressing from start to finish through an interim management assignment.

Over in the Netherlands, putting interim managers into newly privatised enterprises has been a major part of EIM's workload. For instance, the municipality of The Hague has turned its energy programme — electricity and gas generation, town hot water and energy conversion from waste disposal —

over to private hands even though the Dutch capital remains a major shareholder. The new company, GEB, employs 1200 people and serves nearly a quarter of a million householders. It called in EIM and Willem Stoorvogel, a former general manager of Phillips Medical Division to run things while they found a successor and to train him for the job when they did so.

'GEB wasn't in trouble, but it was facing some cultural changes which could have caused problems', says Stoorvogel. Some of them were to do with people. Those who had not gained promotion as a result of privatisation were disappointed and needed to be remotivated and built into a new kind of team — and those who would not go along with the new set-up had to be let go or re-assigned.

New attitudes to energy consumption also created a new agenda for customers. 'In most businesses the aim is to increase sales. What we had to do was to reduce energy consumption, though we were politically constrained in the extent to which we could raise prices.' It was not an easy assignment, though Stormvogel maintains that even here the core tasks were similar to other interim management jobs he had undertaken. Productivity, quality and customer care were the benchmarks. But he admits that he found the regular meetings with the EIM counsellor and other EIM interims a great help. 'Because EIM have been doing a lot of public sector work, there were quite a number of interim managers who had "been there before" and who I could turn to for advice.'

Overall the profile of interim managers in the European Community is similar to those in the USA. The report on the US 'headrenting market' in *Consultants News* (Issue 3, Winter 1989) describes them as

> pre-screened high level professionals, often earning more than $100,000 and no longer saddled with a stigma about temporary work

who fall into the following broad classifications:

- Independent consultants who use interim management firms as one of the channels through which they market their services

- Recycled retirees

- 'Golden parachuters' (an American term for people who have been given a large enough redundancy package to free them from the need to earn a regular income)

- Lifestyle seekers, who want to exchange autonomy and the chance to pick assignments that interest them for the corporate rat race

- Top-notch specialists, for whose talents there is unlikely to be enough consistent demand in any one firm, but for which there is market spread across an industry sector.

> **The typical profile of an interim manager is someone between 45 and 55 with a successful record of senior line management in a respected company**

This corresponds to the position in the UK and the European continent. A survey of interim management firms conducted prior to writing this book shows that most of the individuals on their databanks are 45–55 and have been earning salaries equivalent to ranges of between £40,000 and £80,000 a year. Michael Kelly, a partner in EIM, states 'We operate at the top end of the market, and the majority of managers in our pool had been earning a minimum of £70,000 a year.'

Opening the gates of opportunity

The effective deployment of specialists is a growing area of opportunity for interim managers. Graham Balchin, a mechanical engineer, undertakes interim assignments in the oil, gas and petrochemical industries. They come to him either independently or through GMS Consultants. 'Major contractors are often awarded contracts which call for elements of specialist knowledge which they don't have in-house', he says. 'Bringing in an interim manager is the ideal solution if there is going to be no long-term demand for it.' Another source of work for him is the result of mergers and take-overs. 'Companies find they've accidentally acquired an operation which they know very little about — for instance a process plant which is outside the core activity they have taken over. An interim manager can run it for them and also give an impartial opinion on what best to do with it.'

A good example of a contract which unexpectedly calls for expert knowledge which the contractor cannot supply is provided by the files of Albemarle Interim Management. A company supplying security gates for Heathrow Airport was suddenly asked by the British Airports Authority to provide four level crossing gates, each weighing about 20 tonnes and big enough to allow the passage of Concorde and jumbo jets. The job had to be completed in four months, with a stiff penalty clause if it ran over time.

There were two obvious alternatives. One was saying that they could not do the job — and possibly letting a competitor in on a major contract. The other was to hire a permanent person to handle the contract. But the latter course would have taken precious weeks of recruitment time (which might have been conducted too hastily anyway) and left them with someone for whose specialist skills they would have little long-term use. The answer was to put in an interim as project manager. Using techniques that were particularly suited to this type of assignment, the job was completed on time, despite the exacting specifications set by the client.

PERSONAL CHARACTERISTICS OF SUCCESSFUL INTERIM MANAGERS

Many thousands of managers fall into these categories described on page 39, which explains why interim management firms are besieged with applications from individuals who want to sign up with them. So what characteristics do they look for? Over ten years EIM have identified a number of salient ones:

- Wide management experience in relevant industries, from a generalist, not purely technical standpoint

- A sound management track record which inspires confidence with permanent employees on the site

- Strong analytical and communication skills

- The ability to size up complex problems rapidly and to identify a course of action

- Being able to combine long-term strategic thinking with a keen sense of the importance of measurable results and of getting things done in the short-term

- Being a focused, task-oriented achiever

- Giving consistent leadership, combined with flexibility in reacting to events and circumstances when this is required

- The capacity to transfer knowledge to the permanent workforce at every level

- Interpersonal and motivating skills

- Awareness of political issues, in the corporate sense, coupled with the ability to take a detached view of them

- Physical and mental toughness

- Sufficient personal financial stability to be able to take tough decisions without fear of the assignment being terminated for that reason

[41]

- A strong sense of autonomy and independence — though loners do not make good interim managers. However, successful interim managers are not dependent on popular approval or externally conferred marks of status.

These characteristics add up to what the British call 'a safe pair of hands' — a general impression of soundess and steadiness. It is managers who can command these characteristics, allied to technical skills and competencies, who are singled out by interim management firms.

> **The fact that interim managers are often 'sensibly overqualified' for their assignments means that the learning curve is flattened — and that smaller companies can get access to expertise, part-time, at a level they could not afford full-time.**
>
> *Robert Mark, Partner, EIM*

But oddly enough this itself leads to another client objection. Surely, this one runs, such people are over-qualified for interim management tasks? EIM maintains, however, that the situations into which interim managers are called are generally exceptionally tough ones that need people who would otherwise be considered overqualified for that role. Moreover, in the case of part-time assignments, the interim management concept allows firms, generally small ones, access to high calibre managers whom they would otherwise not be able to afford.

The generic skills of interim managers

Managers who have these characteristics can apply them effectively to challenges that are outside their obvious qualifications and background. Torex Hire, a £4.5m turnover chain of tool hire stores in the West Midlands, decided to diversify into the hire of modular self-erect marquees but ran into trouble over their manufacture. With the peak marquee hiring season coming up, there was no one on the Torex team who could be spared to look after it, and the anticipated scale of operations was not large enough to justify a full-time appointment.

Chief Executive Ben Longrigg approached Barton Interim Management. They suggested John Skinner, a former production and distribution manager, on their books. He went in for a month and sorted out the problem. Longrigg was enthusiastic about the results. 'The great advantages of interim management is that you can get someone to devote the whole of their time, non-stop, to doing the particular project you have in mind. When you're on a tight schedule, the concentration an interim manager can bring to the task can be crucial.'

INTERIM MANAGEMENT AS A STEP TO PERMANENT EMPLOYMENT

Most interim management firms do not see it as a step in this direction. In fact, EIM comes down quite strongly against it, on the grounds that an interim manager cannot act with detachment if he or she has a vested interest in what they are doing, such as an eye to future permanent relationships with people working in the organisation. Moreover, the best manager for the interim period may not be the best person on a permanent basis. Indeed many of EIM's interim managers express the view that 18 months is the maximum time for such an assignment. Longer stays tend to result in interims 'going native', rather than striking the balance between inside commitment and outside detachment.

Certainly, as stated in the first chapter, both interim managers themselves and intermediaries feel that in essence interim management is a career path of its own and that the people who are most successful in it, see interim management in that light. Nevertheless, the fact remains that some interim management assignments are so successful that a full-time job offer is made to the incumbent. Although there is no better way of establishing someone's suitability for a job than actually trying them out in it, such offers are rarely taken up. When they are, the usual practice is to charge the client a fee related to the salary being offered, in much the same way as in a search. However the percentage is usually lower than that applied to search fees.

EXECUTIVE SUMMARY

Interim management is not the same thing as 'temping', even though 'temporary executive' is sometimes the term that is applied to this method of working. However there are superficial similarities in operating procedures, inasmuch as they both offer a short and limited term resource, through a third party which is responsible for pay and administration, and which can be asked to terminate the arrangement whenever the client no longer needs it.

However, the calibre of the people who become interim managers is far higher than that which is associated in most managers' minds with the idea of the 'temp'. Interim managers fall into three principal categories:

- Mid career executives, either general managers or functional/technical specialists, who have decided to go out on their own as independent consultants.

- New age executives in their mid-thirties or early forties who, for family or lifestyle reasons no longer want to be tied to corporate careers.

- Early retired senior managers who still want to play an active, if not a full-time business role.

These people represent not only a valuable resource but an effective way for firms to combine the energy and flexibility of their young high-fliers with the judgement and know-how of their elders — without, however, clogging up their payrolls or blocking up roads to the top.

Interim management attracts a wide variety of people, but all of them have been found to have some characteristics in common. In summary, these could be said to be, in the short-term, what Tom Peters calls 'a bias for action' (top of his list of 'excellent' qualities, incidentally) — that is, coupled with the ability to think the consequences of action through in the long term, with excellent interpersonal and communicating skills and with both physical and mental toughness. It adds up to 'a safe pair of hands'.

These qualities will be effective in any situation. Companies who believe their problems are 'too complicated' for interim management generally have not understood what these problems really are.

REFERENCES

1. According to a survey of some 320 interim managers conducted by GMS Consultancy (The Independent Consultancy Market, 1991) only a minority of interim managers or leased executives describe themselves as such. Almost half prefer to use the term independent consultant. That is probably because the vast majority of them also accept independent assignments, not gained through an interim management intermediary.

2. This point was made in an article in *The Daily Telegraph.* Headed 'Temps Who Can Cost Up To £600 a day', it said 'There is an image problem here. British management tends to think of temporary staff in terms of secretaries or storemen.'

3. It is an open secret among career counselling firms that the head of one successful and high profile British company originally joined it through outplacement from his previous employers.

4. 'When High Fliers Turn Their Backs On Stress', *Personnel Management Plus*, April 1991.

5. 'Spending More Time With The Family', *The Times*, 17 April 1991.

3

The Competitive Advantage of Interim Management

One of the questions that is mostly widely asked about interim management is where the difference lies between this and management consultancy.

It is true that in some ways the two are not far apart. EIM in the Netherlands actually developed out of a management consultancy firm, Boer & Croon. According to their chief executive, G H Boskma, it still passes certain assignments, which it regards as being less suitable for interim management, on to such leading consultancies as McKinsey, PA, Booz Allen, Coopers & Lybrand and KPMG. In fact John Hird of Albemarle Interim Management believes that eventually there will be an increasing amount of overlap between management consultancy and interim management. That makes sense, given the general trend for professional and occupational boundaries to become blurred under the pressure of the deregulation now going on in all developed economies: accountancy practices are getting into management consultancy, law firms are getting involved in some of the traditional areas of accountancy and merchant banking, while venture capital firms are setting up alliances with providers of interim management — to name just a few examples of this process.

Some management consultancies are already operating on certain projects in a way which is similar to interim management firms, by bringing in outside 'associates' to cover areas where they lack some essential specialist skill in-house. Others employ independent consultants on contract part-time in specialist areas for which they do not have a big enough demand to justify a full-time appointment. This is very close to interim management, although from the client's point of view there is one big difference. He pays the charge-out rate for consultancy, which in the UK can be anything from £1000 a day, as compared to the £600–£1000 a day charged by interim management firms for a senior manager.[1]

INTERIM MANAGEMENT AND CONSULTANCY: THE DIFFERENCE EXPERIENCE MAKES

Bringing in outsiders is, for consultancies, a response to one of the challenges that interim management has posed to them. Otherwise, the latter simply do not have the wide range of people to draw from that interim management firms can call up through their database. They also lack consultants with line management experience. In fact the career tracks of line managers and management consultants are quite different and movement between consultancy practices and line management positions, and vice versa, are quite rare.

In part the reasons are financial. Management school graduates are eagerly courted by consultancies and financial services firms, who value the training in analytical skills that a business education brings with it. Industrial companies and firms at the hard edge of the service sector do not rate it quite so highly and are not prepared to pay business graduates the large starting salaries that they can command in these other two sectors. Thus business administration graduates, many of whom have made quite substantial sacrifices by funding their studies, and in some cases giving up a year's earnings to do a full-time course, gravitate towards jobs where rewards are highest.[2] Their intention may be to go into line management after a year or two on a higher income, but in practice that is seldom realised. It is very difficult to move to a lower income bracket once you have acquired a high income habit and the commitments that go with it.

Consultants, a panel of executive search companies warned Harvard Business School graduates at a career development seminar, primarily hang pictures on the wall. They get little opportunity to paint them themselves. Putting it more directly, they have little experience in implementation. Yet this is increasingly what clients demand — some management consultants admit as much. In Andersen Consulting's annual survey,[3] Terry Neill, head of its services division, writes: 'Strategic consultants — often the best and the brightest of the business schools[4] — achieved some real successes . . . Yet as the decade enters its second year, ushering in an increasingly rigorous economic climate, there's growing feeling that something's gone wrong. Too many lofty visions have failed to translate into reality.' In other words clients are now asking for implementation, not just recommendation.

Consultants, in the main, offer recommendation and strategic planning. The role of interim managers is to implement in the short term, but with a view to the long-term interests of the client.

The consultancy practices are aware of that and increasingly claim to be able to offer it. The argument of interim management firms is that they are better placed to do so, because unlike the consultancies, they have senior managers who have made it happen. As Robert Mark of EIM puts it:

'Our managers have been there, where the bullets fly.'

This is not just a question of going one better in order to compete. There are sound practical reasons why interim management firms prefer experienced managers, mainly in the age range 45–55, to younger ones. These reasons are related to the situations which they are called upon to deal with. As we saw in the previous chapter, they are mainly concerned with some form of either crisis management or the management of change. In such circumstances experience tells, because

- The interim manager has to be able to read the play very quickly. He has to know which are likely to be the worst problem areas, and to be able to call for and interpret the information which is likely to throw light on them. Very often, interim managers discover that the real problem is significantly worse than that outlined in the brief.

- There is very little time for analysis. As Winston Churchill used to put it in his memos, 'action this day' is the watchword for at least some aspects to prevent the situation deteriorating.

- The interim manager has to be able to give clear leadership right from the start. In an article in the Drake Business Review[5] which I wrote a couple of years ago, I gave an example of that, which I cannot better. When Montgomery arrived in the Western Desert in 1941, he faced a situation which called for turnaround leadership. On his very first day, he called his staff together and told them what changes he was going to make immediately, what he expected of his subordinates and what he intended to do about the enemy — in military terms, the competition. 'A spirit of hope, at any rate of clarity, was born that day', he wrote in his memoirs.[6]

- The interim manager has to be able to overcome the resistance to change which is found in any organisation. It is a mixture of its people defending their positions,

[50]

justifying their previous actions and fending off change with the Not Invented Here (NIH) reaction.

- The interim manager has to be able to take tough decisions about people. One of the reasons why incumbents find it difficult and stick with bad hiring decisions longer than they should do was identified by R N Bolles, the author of the American best seller, *What Color Is Your Parachute*.[7] Within a very short time, he wrote, the people you hire stop being Mr Smith and Mrs Jones and become John and Betty and that changes your attitude towards them. An interim manager has no such ties with the past and he almost certainly has had experience of letting people go.

Another crucial difference between an interim manager and a management consultant is in the relationship with the client. Management consultants, says Robert Mark of EIM, are the employees of their firm. Its concerns and interests remain paramount and responsibility is to its partners or directors. Interim managers become part of the home team (with the important difference that it is not responsible for financial and administration matters relating to the interim manager). During the assignment they identify totally with its interests, though they also retain their independence so as not to get caught up in its internal politics. An important part of EIM's ongoing role during an assignment is to ensure this independence and objectivity is retained.

> **Management consultants are responsible to their practice. Interim managers are responsible for the success of the assignment.**

This gets more difficult as time goes on and is the reason why interim management companies believe that the maximum term for any assignment should be 18–24 months. The average, in fact, is six to nine months. 'Working yourself out of the job', has been defined as the ideal outcome of an interim management assignment. Spinning out an assignment to generate income is definitely discouraged.

ALTERNATIVES TO INTERIM MANAGEMENT

Interim management, though less expensive than management consultancy, is not a cut price solution. If the all-in costs, including expenses where the interim manager has to stay away from home, come to roughly £4000 a week, one is talking of an outlay of £104,000 on a six-month assignment. That is still extremely cost effective in real terms, a point with which we deal in more detail in Chapter 5, but it is nevertheless a sum which might prompt companies to consider alternatives.

Internal secondment

Internal managers, however good, are not suited to secondment to interim assignments involving crisis or turnaround situations. The likelihood is that even if they are not already involved in the heritage of past decisions, they are much more at risk of being so than someone coming in from the outside.

Succession/promotion try-outs

If there is doubt about the capacity of the 'natural' successor to a position, then trying him or her out in it is not a good solution. For one thing it creates a problem with remuneration. Do you, or do you not, pay the person being tried out the rate for the job if it is higher than his or her current earnings? There is also an expectation that the appointment will eventually be confirmed. If it is not, the effect on the morale of the person concerned will be disastrous, quite apart from the incidental problems that arise if he or she has been awarded a pay increase during tenure. Human resource directors have found that, in such cases, it is far better to advertise the job and to advise potential internal candidates to apply. If finding a successor is likely to be a lengthy process and the job is a key one, it is better to appoint an interim manager while the recruitment process is going.

Using the 'Old Boy' network

The old boy network does have some points in its favour, which, in Britain particularly, are related to the national culture of school, university, sporting and (even) business networks. It does enable managers to obtain rough and informal points of reference on people, but they do not compare with the rigorous selection methods used by interim management firms. Doing someone a good turn, which is often the basis of interim appointments made in this way, is not a sound basis for choosing a turnaround or crisis manager. Even filling in a position pending an appointment or during a temporary period of absence can be a delicate matter which needs a professional touch.

Using an independent consultant, not connected with an interim management company

There are certainly some very competent independents around and they can be cheaper than working through an interim management company. As with any agency, interim management firms add on a cost to the rates of the people they provide. In this context, Michael Kelly of EIM asks clients to consider the quality assurance element that is provided by the rigorous selection processes of interim management firms. In the case of EIM, there is also the added factor that it holds itself liable for performance standards and project manages the assignment all the way through.

The other factor to consider is speed. Advertising for an interim manager and then going through the selection process can take as long as recruiting a full-time executive — assuming that, in the case of specialist jobs, the right person sees the advertisement. By contrast, there is a very good chance that an interim management firm will have someone who fills even an unlikely specification. EIM, for instance, was asked to find an engineer with a working knowledge of German to recommission an oil refinery in north Germany for a British client. The numbers of people available to meet this specification could probably be counted on the fingers of one hand, but it so happened that one of them was on EIM's books.

> **In a crisis, speed is of the essence. An interim manager can be put on board in a matter of days.**

Using one's own non-executive directors

Although non-executive directors have occasionally been used in this role (the writer for one!), the switch from non-executive to executive responsibilities and back again, is not easy to make if the assignment goes much beyond a pure caretaking one. The function of the non-executive is much more like the advisory one of a consultant than that of an implementer.

MANAGEMENT CONSULTANCY AND INTERIM MANAGEMENT: MAKING THE CHOICE

This brings us back full circle to the question of whether there are circumstances where the internal resources of a company need to be augmented by outside help and in which it is in fact better to use a firm of management consultants than an interim management company.

It is likely that when a turnaround is best managed by a team with a strong input of strategic planning skills, management consultants might be a better option. Interim managers are best chosen from the ranks of those with a 'bias for action' and it is unusual to find this combined with the ability to develop detailed long-term strategies. The nature of many interim assignments — 'action this day' plus knowledge transfer — in any case leaves little time for the kind of analysis which is the principal strength of management consultants.

One interim management intermediary which is at the sharp end of making decisions between this and management consultancy is the interim management service of PA Consulting Group. As the name implies, its core business is consultancy. Martin Wood, its director, has no difficulty in deciding when a client needs an interim manager and when someone from his firm's consultancy arm might be a better choice. He sees interim management as essentially 'line consultancy' to be deployed when speed and urgency are paramount considerations. In military terms that might be likened to a tactical situation, as compared to the broader strategic questions which call for the analytical approach of orthodox management consultancy.

A similar dilemma — deciding which assignments should be handled by the management consultancy arm of his firm and which come into the category of interim management — is regularly faced by Derek Wallington of Ernst & Young. He believes that if the client's key requirement is for a team to produce a set of findings which have to be discussed, agreed and only then implemented, that is a management consultancy role. But if he needs swift action, interim management is the only solution.

Yet another situation when it might be better to use an interim manager than a consultant is identified by Bill Penney of P-E International, which also offers both services. In their operation the interim manager's reporting responsibility is to his client, not P-E, an interim might be the best choice in situations where highly confidential or sensitive information needs to be kept within the organisation. This is not a reflection on the discretion of management consultants, but simply a consequence of their reporting responsibilities.

EXECUTIVE SUMMARY

Questions are often asked by clients about differences and similarities between interim management and consultancy — particularly since the latter are increasingly claiming to offer implementation as well as advice. There are also some signs that consultancies, under competitive pressure from interim management, are prepared to cut rates.

The principal differences are:

- The temperament, training and background of interim managers as compared to the majority of consultants.

- The range of expertise that interim management providers can draw on — much wider than all but the largest consultancies.

Management consultants are strong on analytical skills, by virtue of the nature and content of the business school training most of them have undergone. Interim managers are line managers or functional specialists with a track record of having made things happen. They are able to read the play quickly, get things going from day one, offer clear leadership, take tough decisions about people and overcome the natural inertia of organisations. These are qualities born of experience.

They also have a different relationship with clients. They become members of the client team, whereas the allegiance of consultants is ultimately with their employers. Their employers' interests are paramount.

There are, however, some circumstances where management consultants are preferable, or at least preferred to interim managers. In the main these are situations which call for heavy input of skills in long-term planning, since interim managers are more likely to concentrate on firefighting roles rather than on plans to improve the water supply to the hydrants.

Nevertheless clients do have some options for managing

change, or crisis or making interim appointments. They can use internal secondments, the old boy network, independent consultants, their own non-executive directors or make trial appointments from their existing staff. None of these options, however, is subjected to the same rigorous matching of managers to situations as the selection process used by interim management firms.

REFERENCES

1. Rates vary according to the location of the job and the level of the job.

2. A British Institute of Management Survey shows 90 per cent of MBA holders 'had made sacrifices in order to study for their qualification', 63 per cent said these sacrifices were financial. Half of the respondents had paid for their own fees and 15 per cent had taken out loans to cover them.

3. View '91.

4. He might also have added, the most highly paid. According to a survey produced for MBA graduates, the free income per professional in UK strategy firms was between £100,000 and £200,000.

5. Anyone Can Be A Leader, *Drake Business Review* vol. 3, no. 2.

6. Quoted by Nigel Hamilton in *Monty: The Making Of A General*, Hamish Hamilton, London 1981.

7. Bolles, R N, *What Color Is Your Parachute*, Ten Speed Press.

4

The Right Stuff of Interim Management

There is enormous interest in interim management on the part of individual executives who want to move to this method of working and away from traditional ideas of a job. That is supported both by social trends towards greater autonomy and economic ones towards more flexible ways of working. The Sunday Telegraph[1] has estimated that in the UK by the year 2000, only half the workforce of 26 million will be in full-time paid employment, as compared to 67 per cent in 1990. Fifty per cent of the rest will be in 'other paid employment'. It is likely that a very high proportion of them will be managers. According to the Institute of Manpower Studies, even now (1991) 38.2 per cent of managers in Britain are self-employed, as compared to a total of around 12 per cent for the workforce as whole.[2]

These figures are confirmed by anecdotal evidence. Michael Kelly of Executive Interim Management has seen 20,000 CVs since EIM started in 1987 and still gets about 250 per week.

When I first wrote about interim management in *The Sunday Times* that year, the firms that I mentioned received literally thousands of letters from managers wanting more information. It was noticed that although some of these were from people looking for jobs, a significant number came from executives who were securely employed. In fact several were from main board directors of nationally known PLCs.

MAKING THE CHOICE: PRE-SELECTION

Looking at interim management from the point of view of these individuals, how do the providers of this service make their choice from the enormous number of potential candidates they hear from? That is an important question, not only for them but also for clients who want to be assured about quality control.

Practices vary somewhat, but it has to be said that comparatively few of those who want to be interim managers are chosen to go on the database of the intermediaries. EIM for instance, says that only about 150 of the 20,000 managers who have contacted it, have been selected as suitable. That is because EIM has pursued a strategy of being a niche player at the top end of the market. It focuses on chief executives and high level functional specialists. Another factor that makes EIM particularly selective is its policy of taking full financial responsibility for the contract. Other interim management firms do not go this far, though they do urge interims to take out professional indemnity insurance, and this has much the same effect. The reason why this is necessary in the UK is that there is a legal liability under the Supply of Goods And Services Act of 1982 that anyone who offers a service should be competent to do so. By implication an interim manager, or indeed any consultant, making a mistake which cost his client money, could lay himself open to legal action on grounds of incompetence.

In effect EIM audits this competence in selecting interim managers. A good many CVs are rejected at the outset. As is also the case with job applications, those that fail the 'first impression' test are poorly presented physically, too long (they should not be more than three pages, at the outside), contain crass spelling mistakes, omit vital information (amazingly, some CVs do not give an address) or contain unexplained career gaps. Francis Howard of Stream Resources also eliminates people who he knows from experience that he cannot place, either because they are too specialised or too junior, or too far above the upper age limit within which interim management largely operates.

> In considering CVs sent in by prospective interim managers, intermediaries look primarily for evidence of previous assignments, either in independent consultancy — or failing that — in previous projects carried out successfully which resemble interim management assignments.

There is also the issue of relevance. Interim management assignments are different from the traditional idea of a 'job', therefore CVs that have been produced for job applications will not do. Interim management firms are looking for different criteria from those of employers. Above all they are looking for evidence of previous interim or independent consultancy assignments that have been successfully completed; or, in the absence of that, any project that the applicant has carried out which resembles interim management-like tasks. They are less bothered about age up to about 55 — there have even been interim management appointments where the candidate was over 60.

As far as the details of a mainstream career are concerned, as with employers, they focus on what has been quantitatively achieved in the course of the career, but they are also interested in the circumstances. Bearing in mind the often delicate context in which an interim manager will have to work, and which have been indicated in the previous two chapters, they will be looking at achievements in the light of:

- interpersonal skills;

- a record of managing change successfully, rather than a range of *status quo* jobs;

- the ability to work autonomously (that much used term 'self starter'). Also, as stated earlier, interim managers are not people whose performance is dependent on the approval of others. The Birmingham-based firm Praxis is unusual in employing psychometric tests to evaluate such factors;

- depth of line management experience in a variety of settings and preferably of companies. A point made by Cees Boer, one of the founders of BCG, is that if one is likely to be assigned to different companies as an interim manager, it obviously helps if one's corporate experience has prepared one for variety;

- degree of profit responsibility;

- evidence of willingness to be mobile — in the nature of interim management, assignments can occur anywhere in the country and may involve being away from home during the week.

Some of these criteria are, of course, no different from those demanded in any position, but interim management firms are more interested in motivation. They want to know what prompts an executive to become an interim manager, and there are some answers which produce a negative reaction. The most common ones, says EIM's Michael Kelly are: 'something to do while I'm looking around for a permanent job' and 'heard a lot about it, want to try it out'. John Hird of Albemarle looks for evidence of applicants becoming interim managers 'of their own free will' which presumably means that he is less favourably disposed to those who see it as an alternative to redundancy — or at any rate who say so openly. Interim management firms also look positively on candidates who can be articulate about their motivation to tackle important issues, achieve measurable results, transfer owner-ship of the means of doing so and who then want to move on.

Kelly is convinced that only those who have made a commitment to interim management as a way of working are likely to be a success at it.

They also look discreetly for some evidence of the ability to sustain that commitment. Interim managers are by no means assured of continuous work by being on the database of an interim management provider. Few of them get more than six months' worth a year from any one such firm, though in quite a number of cases they fill gaps in assignments coming from that source by also working independently. In most cases they are also registered with more than one interim management/ executive leasing firm — one interim manager interviewed said he was on the register of no less than nine intermediaries. Interim management firms pay no retainers and neither expect nor require exclusive rights to the services of managers on their databank. In other words, taking on interim management assignments should be seen as just one aspect of a wider marketing plan for the independent consultant — though once a full-time assignment is under way, they would be prevented from taking on other work.

The subject of contracts with the various stakeholders in an interim management situation is dealt with more fully in Appendix 4, but the point we want to make here is that although interim management is well paid (EIM's average daily rate of between £600–£1200 is somewhat higher than the industry average because of the level of the assignments on which it has focused), intermediaries like to take on people who will not be distracted by financial pressures, and who will not (as some management consultants are accused of having been) be tempted to spin out assignments because of the need to maintain fee levels.

Though the principles are broadly the same, other companies use different approaches to preselection. Some, for instance, send an application form to candidates whose letter and CV look potentially interesting. AIMS's (Albemarle Interim Management Services) form calls for the following details. They are interesting both as an indication, both to potential clients and potential interim managers, of the kind of record they are looking for:

- the length of time the applicant has operated as an independent consultant;

- age and qualifications;

- languages spoken;

- countries in which the applicant has worked;

- assignment disciplines and positions in which the applicant would be interested;

- three relevant appointments that the applicant has held: position, industry, company, turnover;

- three relevant independent assignments that the applicant has completed: position, industry, company, turnover;

- special skills (eg knowledge of JIT procedures);

- normal daily fee rate;

- readiness to work away from home or even overseas;

- references.

But what happens in a less than ideal world? Interim management firms prefer people who are already operating as independents. It is a cardinal principle of selection that advertisements specify the ideal, but often have to compromise. Carl Hague of Praxis makes the point that there is an increasing number of good and able managers coming on to the market as the result of corporate downsizing and many of these would make good interims. The critical factors he identifies in this respect are:

- family circumstances — whether the spouse is likely to be able to handle the uncertainties of independence and what the attitude of the family would be to potentially prolonged periods of absence from home. A factor here would be the age of the children and the degree of dependence of aged relatives;

- other commitments — people involved in ongoing activities in the community are not suitable, nor are those who, for whatever reason, might not be able to respond to take on an assignment in, say, Munich, within a matter of days;

- personal health;

- self confidence;

- ability to handle stress and pressure;

- the degree of ambition;

- languages — because of the growing importance of the single market he looks for bi- and preferably trilinguals;

- ability to market themelves convincingly;

- ability and integrity-related references.

GMS adds a further important point (and warning) in its *Guide to Executive Leasing*:

> The independent who does not have his own micro-computer and is unable to perform basic functions on computers will increasingly be seen as inert and out of date.

MAKING THE CHOICE: PRELIMINARY INTERVIEWS

Reference checking is also stressed by EIM, where it is regarded as an integral part of the preliminary interview process. In the preliminary interviews — EIM's Michael Kelly says they conduct at least two — potential interims are asked what they have actually done and what they have achieved in those positions. They are then further quizzed about who could validate these claims.

> Interim management firms are not looking for character references from the great and the good, but nitty-gritty affirmations from the people prospective interims have worked for.

The lesson for interviewees here, irrespective of the intermediaries whom they have approached, is that firms are not looking for character references from the great and the good, but nitty-gritty stuff from people they have worked for or with. References are likely to be taken up by telephone rather than in writing. This is common practice among experienced recruiters in any role, because a more truthful answer will emerge in response to live questions than in a written document where referees are sometimes deterred by the possibilities of libel.

The issues explored in the preliminary interview, which are confirmed by reference validation, resemble those covered in the AIMS questionnaire:

Career

In view of the tasks likely to be faced by an interim manager, interim management providers tend to look for executives in the age range 50–55. They should have reached a level that will result in the interim manager actually being, in one sense, 'over-qualified' for the job he may be asked to do, either because implementation will be unusually tough or (in the case of part-time assignments) because the whole rationale is that the client is being offered a more high powered person than he could have on his payroll. A £2m–£3m turnover business is hardly likely to be able to afford a £70,000 a year finance director full-time — but it could afford, and might benefit

[66]

immensely from, such a person as a one or two day a week part-timer.

Experience

Directly relevant experience at this stage is not the issue because it is unusual that the provider will actually have an assignment for the interim at the preliminary stage. Only then is it an advantage, though not necessarily a decisive one. Far more important are his competencies as a manager, the responsibilities he had in previous jobs and the evidence that he was able to 'make it happen'.

The size of the organisations he has worked for

This is important because when an assignment does come up, the interim should have had experience in an operation of at least equivalent size. The reason is that large and small organisations operate differently and have different cultures. However, some interim management firms say that managers with large company background find it difficult to adapt to the 'head cook and bottle washer' culture of the smaller enterprise.

Place of residence

This is a bigger consideration in the UK than it is in, say, the Netherlands, where a high proportion of businesses are within fairly easy reach of each other and of the main residential areas. An interim manager living in the London area would have to stay on site on an assignment in the south-west. That could add considerably to the cost for the client, as he is generally expected to meet such expenses.

Some further considerations governing the choice of people who are taken seriously as contenders for interim management positions are implied in a survey of the independent consultancy market in the UK, produced by GMS Consultancy Ltd.[3]

[67]

It identifies a number of features that characterise 'the successful senior executive operating on a freelance basis'. That is essentially what interim managers are doing, so it is likely that at least implicitly interim management/leased executive providers look for those same characteristics in evaluating CVs and interviews:

- Having a 'trade'. GMS believes that excellence can usually only be achieved in a narrow range of specialities

- Having kept technical knowledge up to date through training. It has been estimated that the 'half-life' of most qualifications now is five years; ie half of what one has learned is out of date five years later

- Awareness of what is happening in the business environment at large

- Good physical appearance

- Good presentation techniques, both written and verbal. Promotional material, says GMS, 'should be simple, factual, beautifully presented without being over-glossy.'

- Emotional stability.

MATCHING THE PERSON TO THE JOB

Although clients want to make an appointment in a hurry, they also need to get the right person for the job. The strength of interim management firms is that if they have a well-maintained databank of quality executives, the likelihood is that that person can be quickly identified, though practice varies as to how this is done. At EIM the process is based on a second set of interviews, based on details which have emerged from the preliminary ones.

At Ernst & Young the procedure is triggered off by a computer search against the qualities that emerge from the job specification. That is then gradually narrowed down to a short-list of four to six people which is presented to the client. Derek Wallington says that sometimes the client asks him to be present at the interview and even to suggest what their choice should be. He does not think this is a good idea, again on the grounds that the client must be committed to the interim, and vice versa.

At EIM the process is different. Instead of producing a short-list, the firm itself selects the interim manager for the assignment, on the basis of a very detailed job specification which has been agreed with the client. From that is developed a profile of the kind of individual that the assignment calls for, in terms of preferred qualifications, experience and personal attributes. The interim manager who fits the job specification is then identified from data on EIM's database, and re-interviewed. He is checked out by the client, but primarily to ensure that the 'personal chemistry' works, since all the preliminaries have already been agreed between EIM and its client.

A typical case was that of a financial appointment which called for a man with an accounting qualification who was also a persuasive presenter because he would have to win the hearts and minds of his colleagues in getting their help in dealing with a crisis. Experience had to include treasury management and a successful negotiating record with financial institutions in a similar setting, while technical skills were to be a knowledge of computer systems and taxation.

These would, in fact, have been very similar to the desirable attributes set out in a job advertisement — except that the interim management provider could produce them very much more quickly. However, speed in preparing the job and person specification has to be reconciled with accuracy. In carrying out this task interim management companies have to be extremely skilled readers of the corporate situation in both the technical and cultural sense. The reason is that the interim manager does not have time for analysis once he gets on site. At least the general outlines of the situation should have been sized up for him if he is to be effective from day one. Equally, the client does not have the time to go through a long induction process. The ability to 'prepare the battlefield', the importance of which was so clearly demonstrated in the Gulf War, is perhaps the most important quality which interim management/executive leasing firms are able to offer their clients.

EXECUTIVE SUMMARY

There is a growing social trend towards self-employment among managers which coincides with companies moving towards smaller core teams of permanent executives. This is reflected in the large numbers of CVs received by interim management companies. Only a relatively small number of these are selected for serious consideration when an assignment comes up.

The criteria are in many ways similar to those used in sifting job applications, although the emphasis is different. Interest focuses on the individual's commitment to the concept of interim management as a way of life.

In screening CVs and applications for work on interim assignments, intermediaries look for track record, experience, qualifications and current state of knowledge.

When an interim management company is notified of an assignment coming up, developing a job specification is crucial because in the nature of the situation, the individual who is appointed will not have time for analysis. At the same time his personal specification has to be matched to the job. The process is, of course, similar to ordinary search and selection, but it has to be carried out much more quickly. It is possible to put an interim manager into a post within a week, but speed has to be combined with care. The ability to reconcile, as the product of experience, what are often regarded as conflicting requirements is another chief benefit interim management firms can offer.

REFERENCES

1. *Sunday Telegraph*, 28 October 1990.

2. Meager, N (1991) *Self-Employment In the United Kingdom*, Institute of Manpower Studies, Brighton.

3. The Independent Consultancy Market, GMS, Dunstable, 1990.

5

The Corporate Benefits of Interim Management

One of the objections often raised by clients in talking to interim management companies is that of cost. According to an article in the *Daily Telegraph*,[1] they add around 40 per cent to the fee actually paid to the interim manager. At the very top level one is talking of daily rates approaching those of the major consultancies, but anecdotal evidence suggests firstly that rates are negotiable and secondly that £400–£500 is a more usual figure. In that range, the total cost to the client is between £650–£850 per day.

To a smaller company that may still sound expensive — sometimes on not entirely rational grounds. Addressing a recent conference of independent consultants organised by GMS, one interim manager told of discussions he had had with a small measuring instruments company which was losing £10,000 a month. The speaker suggested (in this case he was operating as an independent) that he should come in on an interim contract to implement a solution which would return it to profit within a year at a total cost of £50,000. That included purchasing and training staff in the use of new equipment which would substantially reduce labour costs. The company turned him down because he was 'too expensive'.

INTERIM MANAGEMENT AND PERMANENT STAFF: COMPARING REAL COSTS

On any reckoning which takes real costs into account, interim managers come out much cheaper than permanent staff. EIM makes the point, echoed by all firms in the industry, that the true costs of a permanent member of staff is about twice their actual salary when you consider all the add-ons, such as:

— pension
— national insurance
— medical insurance
— staff and public holidays
— sickness
— training
— administration
— recruitment cost
— company car.

Interim managers are responsible for their own arrangements in every one of these respects — and they are only paid for days worked. Even discounting the last item, figures produced by Reed Employment show that the total cost of these items adds 55.25 per cent to a salary.[2] Admittedly Reed were talking of office temps, but there is no reason to believe that the situation differs in the case of more senior personnel. Indeed, it could well be balanced even more strongly in the direction of interim managers, if you take further into account the cost of bonuses

[74]

and share option schemes as well as termination.* It is, for instance, particularly hard to attract an executive to manage a turnaround, with all the career hazards that entails — not to mention the intense commitment that is required — without offering him an equity stake.

> The cost of bringing in an interim manager must be weighed, not against the salaries of job incumbents at a similar level, but at the true amount someone on the payroll costs the company — about twice their apparent salary figure.

Leaving that issue aside, though, the cost of an interim manager must also be seen in the context of the fact that he has to meet all these costs himself.

INTERIM MANAGEMENT: THE COMPETITIVE ADVANTAGE

There are also quite a number of further factors which have an indirect bearing on costs and which reinforce the argument that hiring an interim in the situations outlined in previous chapters often makes a lot more sense.

● There is an opportunity as well as a direct cost attached to recruitment. While the process is going on, management time is taken up with filling in while a search or recruitment campaign is going on. Even when an executive search company is employed, at the final stage of the search, management will have to devote a lot of time to interviewing the short-listed candidates. Interim management, of course,

---

* However, some interim managers in Holland reported having received bonuses at the end of a particularly successful assignment.

also involves carefully specifying the assignment with the interim management company. But a more limited palette of attributes is called for from an appointee who is not going to be a permanent member of the company and the whole process is much quicker: 7–14 days.

- As well as providing a fast start in a situation where there is often no time to lose, interim management largely eliminates the induction period that can be so distracting for a permanent appointee. A comment made by an American venture capitalist, Martin S Orland, in a report produced by the American interim management firm, IMCOR, puts the case well:

  Turnarounds call for keen focus and tremendous concentration. They admit and tolerate no distractions. Permanent replacements, in contrast, tend to be distracted. They are often taking leave of long-time colleagues and friends; they are usually feeling out the politics of the new organisation; they may be selling one house, buying another and helping their families adjust to a new environment.

- People who choose to become interim managers — and the issue of free choice is one of the key criteria used by interim management companies — have a different set of attitudes from those who look for permanent employment. They are not seeking stability and safety, nor are they making moves with one eye to future relationships within the organisation. That makes them more prepared to take an objective view of the situation and to come up with the radical solutions that are often required.

- Radical solutions are not, of course, the preserve of interim managers. Management consultants can and do offer them as well. The difference is that interim managers, though objective in their attitudes, do have the wealth of line experience to know what is and is not practicable in real life. What happens, says Orland, is that:

> their experience and industry depth gives them the
> self-confidence to demand and accept the authority to
> get the job done . . . They are not coming in to be 'yes'
> men, or to do a lot of handholding. Rather, they want
> to move decisively, to take a direction that makes
> some sense. But they are experienced enough to avoid
> precipitate action.

Managing a closedown

Closedowns, involving parts of a company or organisation are
among the most difficult situations a manager has to face.
Unless it is done with great skill there may be a loss of external
confidence in the whole company by its market and its
bankers, as well as of morale internally. That was the problem
of an assignment which EIM was asked to tackle. It involved
the closedown of one unprofitable company in a group of
three UK subsidiaries of a Dutch publishing firm. Some
activities and operations would be kept going, while others
would be closed down or sold off.

The task was to implement the latter, without ruining the
standing of the former in terms of asset values and also losing
the staff the company wanted to keep. In these circumstances,
EIM was brought in, because it was felt that the necessary
clarity, direction and commitment could only come from
someone who was seen both externally and internally as being
able to wield the axe without having one to grind, and who
would be able to take an utterly objective view of the situation.
That person could only come from outside, and on an interim
basis — in this case around six months.

The key tasks were identified as:

● the management of the company's human resources in a
way that would both effect the necessary changes and keep

people motivated in a situation that would affect the careers of many of their fellow workers;

- financial management, budgeting and asset valuation in a situation riddled with imponderables;

- continuing liaison with the parent Dutch company and with the managers of the other British subsidiaries to whom human and physical assets being retained were to be transferred.

EIM reports that the project was successfully completed on a budget which fell well below the contingency figure which had been set aside for it.

Interim management can put a highly qualified person part-time into an organisation that could not afford his services full-time. Nicky Cutts of Barton Interim Management gives not-for-profit organisations as a prime example of this. In one case she put in an interim manager as a fund raiser on a 20-hour week. The duration of the assignment was made dependent on reaching specified financial targets.

Appointments made in haste often lead, as has been said of marriages in similar circumstances, to repentance at leisure. Putting in an interim manager allows the board time to look for a permanent replacement. At the same time, the interim manager will be in a position to observe and report on what the situation really is, what qualities a permanent appointee will need to have and what challenges he or she will be facing.

This is important because it has often been noted by search and selection consultants that the nature of a position is altered by its last incumbent and the environment that has been created around him by his management style, his qualities and his cognitive strengths and weaknesses. Unless management is aware of this factor, when the job is advertised it will be built round the previous job specification rather than the present situation.

When a new permanent appointment does not 'work out' —

and that is not an infrequent event in organisations that are in any case in a state of turmoil or when the way ahead is not clear — the cost of making a new appointment is very high. It has been calculated to be as much as two years' salary for the post in question, taking into account severance compensation (which itself can be high where a generous contract of employment has been offered to attract what initially appeared to be the right candidate), re-advertising the job, induction and opportunity cost. One of the main advantages of an interim appointment is that if it goes wrong, it can be terminated very simply and without penalty. The notice required can be as little as a week, though in contracts that have been running for some time or were expected to do so, a month is more common.

> **Interim management offers a unique combination of speedy action while giving companies a breathing space in which to consider their options for the future.**

This naturally leads to the question of of liability if something *does* go wrong. Legally that depends on the status of the interim management company. EIM, for example, are principal contractors offering a service and as such they accept full liability towards the client. Firms which act as agents, on the other hand, do not accept responsibility for work done, though in the main keep track of assignments by maintaining regular contact with both interim managers and clients. Interim managers are also strongly recommended to take out Professional Indemnity insurance against legal liability arising out of work done.[3]

THE TRIPLE ALLIANCE: INTERIM MANAGERS, INTERMEDIARIES AND CLIENTS

Failures in interim management assignments are, by all accounts, rare. This is partly a reflection of the very high quality of the people selected to go into the databanks of interim management/executive leasing providers, but it is also a product of experience gained by them of the kind of people that make good interim managers. An article on the subject in Forbes Magazine sums it up neatly:

> Generally speaking, they have ten years' experience in a high level management position, sufficient financial security to wait for an assignment that truly interests them, a record unblemished by poor performance and a willingness to move (75 per cent of assignments involve temporary relocation).[4]

In Europe too, it has been found that only line executives dedicated to independence are likely to be successful in the role of interim managers.

The fact is that the role is not an easy one, because in addition to the challenges of the assignment itself, the relationship between interim management company, interim manager and client is itself complex. Consider:

- The **interim management company** does not employ the person placed in the assignment, even though he has a contractual relationship with him and will generally have negotiated terms with the client on his behalf.

- The **interim manager** is part of the client's management team, is often appointed to its board of directors but, although he works for the client, he is not in any sense an employee of the client organisation. It is important that the interim manager should understand the corporate culture and to some extent use it as a guideline for action, but he is not part of it, nor is he part of the client organisation's social network. In fact he probably should not be, if he is to remain impartial.

- Where the interim management company is a principal contractor, the **client organisation** has a contractual relationship with the said company. In the case of an agency, this will go no further than the provisions laid down in the Employment Agencies Act or its equivalent in other countries — in other words it will not specify performance in the same way as a contractor relationship is likely to do.

> The interim manager's pride in doing the job well itself means that the client company will not have to be heavily involved in supervision. It can get on with planning for the future.

At the same time, the client company will not be able to offer the same career inducements, penalties and constraints that it would be able to hold out to a member of its staff. Given the fact that so many interims have a successful career behind them and are at least to some extent financially secure, the only real hold it has over an interim manager is his own pride in doing the job well and the commitment made by the interim management company. However the interim management firm does have a valuable input in mediating when conflicts arise — and preferably sooner than that. EIM's Robert Mark warns, speaking of dealing with interim managers: 'The bigger and better they are, the tougher they are to manage.'

IDENTIFYING THE REAL PROBLEMS

A number of interim management firms make the point that interim managers are in a better position to identify real, underlying problems than permanent members of staff. This is not only because a fresh eye always sees more than one which has stopped noticing what has become familiar — such as a badly laid out working area — especially when that eye is linked, as it is in the case of interim managers, to an experienced brain. It is also because, in the nature of interim appointments, members of the permanent staff are more likely to be open with interims about the problems as they see them.

[81]

These problems can cover a wide range of items, from inefficient working practices to interpersonal relationships.

> Because the interim manager has no permanent 'political' role in the organisation, permanent staff are more prepared to be open with him about what they see as the company's, or their own, real problems.

They are less likely to discuss such things with someone who has been appointed to a permanent position, because in the latter situation they will have their eye on the long-term political implications of what they are saying. The presence of an interim is a chance to get things off their chest, to clear the air. They could, of course, do the same thing with a management consultant. The difference is that the presence of the interim manager also means that problem will be tackled because his role is to implement, not merely to report. But Sir Ian McGregor warns that top management may have to be prepared to accept criticisms of their own role as a result of this process, which is why commitment at top level is so important.

But how can an interim manager know that this commitment really exists? There is one simple rule of thumb: the amount he can spend on corporate matters without referral back. That is one of the key points on which the management of the client company will have to make a decision in consultation with the interim management provider. While the interim manager may be empowered to act as he thinks fit — and spend purely as his experience and knowledge of company finances dictate — he may be constrained by this agreement, and therefore (depending on the job concerned) will be aware of his implementation limitations from the outset.

CONFIDENTIALITY

The other question that sometimes worries clients is that of confidentiality. EIM actually embargoes interim managers on its assignments from working for a client in the same industry for twelve months. Other firms take the view that confidentiality is not an issue at the level of integrity at which interim managers operate — any more than it is if a firm retains the services of a reputable firm of management consultants.

KEY FACTORS IN ASSESSING AN INTERIM MANAGEMENT COMPANY: A CHECKLIST

— How quickly and at what level have they responded to your initial enquiry?

— How long have they been in business in that role?

— Who have been their clients?

— What and how large have these clients' business activities been?

— What procedures does the firm use to select interim managers for its database?

— Have any of their interims been asked to stay on in some capacity after the end of the assignment?

— What percentage of the fee goes back to the interim manager?

— How much time was taken to get the brief on the job in question?

— Did they confirm it in writing and was their assessment of the situation accurate and intelligent?

— How long will it be before they produce a short-list?

— Are the shortlisted candidates appropriately qualified and experienced at the right level?

— Are they able to make a prompt start?

— Is the firm an agency or a contractor?
— What arrangements have been made about professional indemnity insurance?

EXECUTIVE SUMMARY

The cost of using interim management is sometimes regarded as high. However, interim managers work out much cheaper than permanent staff when one takes into account real costs such as pensions, insurances etc.

It enables an organisation to use a highly qualified person part-time, which could not afford his services full-time. An interim manager can also serve as a stop-gap while a permanent replacement is sought, without the need to make a hasty, and possibly unsuitable, appointment.

Permanent staff are often more prepared to talk to the interim manager about the company or their own problems, because he has no permanent role in the organisation.

Confidentiality is not regarded as an issue at the level of integrity at which interim managers operate, although some intermediaries have drawn up a code of conduct.

REFERENCES

1. Temps Who Can Cost Up To £600 A Day, 28 October 1990.

2. Godfrey Golzen, *Using Temps Effectively*, Reed Employment, 1988.

3. A Professional Indemnity Plan prepared by the brokers Robert Barrow has been approved by the Association of Temporary And Interim Managers and a proposal form is included in Appendix 4.

4. Rent-an-exec, Forbes, 22 February 1990.

6

Why Not Go It Alone? — Interim Management Versus Independent Consultancy

In invoicing the client, the interim management company can add his overhead of about 40 per cent to the sum he pays over to the consultant he is putting in place — or, if one prefers to put it another way, he takes 40 per cent of the consultant's money. That naturally raises the question among many independent consultants: why not go it alone, and either charge the client less or collect bigger fees? There is some evidence that, at least in the UK, quite a lot of them take this view. No one knows the exact size of the independent consultancy market, but according to a survey produced by GMS it is thought to be worth about £100 million a year in fee value. However, only around 16 per cent of this is being generated by interim management companies, even though there have been sharp increases in the last two years in the numbers of executives registering their names with such intermediaries.[1]

It is however clear from talking to many interim managers that they do not regard this and independent consultancy assignments as an 'either, or' choice; rather they see it as a 'both, and' one. Sometimes they operate independently, at other times they take on interim management assignments through an intermediary. Indeed interim management firms encourage this trend, partly because they make it clear that only a small minority of people can expect a fairly continuous flow of work from them, and partly because operating independently is also a sign of commitment to this as a workstyle.

THE INDIVIDUAL ADVANTAGES OF INTERIM MANAGEMENT

Nevertheless there are some clear advantages in working through an interim management company and it is these which justify, both directly and indirectly, the commissions they charge.

Marketing

The biggest problem faced by independents is marketing. Partly it is a matter of technique. People wth a background in marketing a service or with general management experience in this sphere are generally quite good at it, but those from a products environment find it much more difficult. Managers with purely technical or functional skills find it more difficult still. They have never had to market anything, least of all themselves and are apt to make the most basic mistakes.

At a recent GMS Conference on independent consultancy one obviously very able interim manager with an engineering background told of the humiliating and alarming experience of starting his independent career by sending out hundreds of letters and making dozens of phone calls without getting a single positive response. He has since gone on to make a lot of money, but he had to learn marketing the hard way. It was clear from his presentation that he had an aptitude for it; a gift which not everybody possesses.

> Being on the databank of an interim management company means that the interim working on an assignment can concentrate on the task in hand, knowing that at least some of his marketing is in good hands.

The other factor is time. Marketing is very time-consuming. It is also very difficult to run one full-time assignment while looking for the next one and nothing is more unpopular with clients than an interim manager who has his eye off the ball — or even worse, who is taking or making 'phone calls to other prospective clients in company time.

Thus, almost *the* principal advantage that operating through an interim management firm offers is that of marketing. Many of them operate in tandem either with executive search companies (for example, EIM who work with Egon Zehnder) or management consultancy firms (PA Executive Leasing, Ernst & Young, P–E International) or selection firms (Albemarle, Barton). These relationships are also a source of direct and indirect leads to interim management assignments.

Credibility

The issue of credibility is another one that faces independent consultants, except in the rare cases where they happen to be personally known to a client. Coming to an organisation through an intermediary who is already well-known, with whose firm or with whose associate companies the client may well have done business before and who is known to validate his pool of interims rigorously, is a great advantage in credibility terms.

Fee negotiations

Negotiating fees is a matter that many independents admit to finding difficult. (Incidentally, it is said by selection consultants in general that job candidates are almost universally bad at negotiating their remuneration.) Most interim management companies undertake this process for their clients. Generally speaking, they are in a better position to assess going rates. This may drive down some unrealistic expectations held by independents, and possibly secure them assignments they would not have got at the rates they were thinking of quoting. It is more likely, however, that interim management intermediaries will secure better rates by advancing some of the arguments about the basis of fees outlined in the previous chapter.

Securing Payment

It is in the nature of many interim assignments, especially those concerned with turnarounds, that they involve business risks when it comes to payment. Many, though not all, intermediaries take on this risk themselves and pay interim managers on a monthly basis, irrespective of whether any payment has been received from the client. Some interim management firms can, in fact, point to painful losses incurred where clients on the verge of insolvency could not be pulled back from the brink.

The Social Factor

There is also another dimension to the relationship between interim managers and intermediaries which is significant. One of the problems faced by all independent consultants is that of intellectual as well as physical isolation. GMS helps to counter this by holding an annual conference at which broad issues relating to independent consultancy are addressed, both by outside speakers and by those who are themselves working as independents, and at which they can also talk informally among each other.

EIM lays great emphasis on maintaining contact between interim managers through regular meetings out of working hours. This goes as far as having three annual meetings to exchange ideas and information. These are supplemented by group meetings relevant to specific industries and sectors which can also be attended by any EIM interim. Another feature is annual get-togethers, simply for social purposes.

Networking

The social side of these contacts also has a very direct business relevance. The concept of 'networking' is coming into widespread business use, as hierarchies are replaced by flatter organisational structures. It means that instead of processes and projects being carried out on a top down, command and control model, they are increasingly being handled by networks and teams of people with complementary skills, who call on each other to contribute ideas and skills as and when these are needed. Within interim management firms networks have formed, sometimes formally, sometimes informally, of independent consultants who work together on this basis. There is also a great deal of reassurance in knowing that where you cannot tackle all the aspects of an assignment, you can nevertheless take it on in the secure knowledge that there are members of the network who can complement your own qualifications, experience and skills.

CLIENT PROCEDURES

Bringing an assignment to a successful conclusion depends more than anything else on establishing a satisfactory relationship right from the outset with the client. Merlin Alty, a highly successful interim manager who has worked independently as well as through EIM, sees 'clear objectives' as being paramount. At the same time he warns against too many details being put into the job specification. Like many other interims, his experience has been that the real nature of the problem is often different from (and sometimes worse than) that outlined by the client organisation. There must therefore be room for manoeuvre.

The other factor that he and others highlight is the importance of top-level commitment within the organisation to the concept of interim management and to the interim manager himself. If this is not evident, there is indeed the danger that the interim will be treated as a glorified, if highly paid, temp. What he says will not be what goes, there will be constant appeals to higher authority on the controversial decisions that are often necessary in the situation that interim managers often find and even where they are carried out, it may well be in a token way. Alty recommends that within the first couple of days the interim manager should be personally introduced by the chief executive or chairman to all the people he will be working with directly. Notwithstanding the need for action, this is an essential preliminary to making it happen.

> **Interim management firms have wide experience of the factors critical to the success of an assignment — they extend beyond the obvious ones of functional competence.**

One of the virtues of working with an interim management provider is that they have experience of the factors critical to the success of an assignment and are able to guide the interim manager in the right directions in his discussions with clients. In some cases they are prepared to sit in on such discussions either at the preliminary stage or when disputes and difficulties arise. EIM has produced a number of guidelines for interim managers. They relate to crisis management, but they are broadly applicable to a spectrum of situations in which interim management is deployed. Beginning with the advice to 'acquire sufficient powers before you start' — which, as we have indicated earlier, depends on securing strong and visible commitment at the top of the organisation, it goes on to list the following considerations which interim managers should bear in mind[2]:

- Your reading of the situation, how you will operate, how they will operate, the controls you will improve immediately on cash, contracts etc.

- Get top level commitment to the recovery plan

- Set out the financial basis for your recovery plan and make clear your determination to deviate from it only in exceptional circumstances.

- Agree the communication structure which will be necessary to get its messsage across, as well as dealing efficiently with day to day management logistics.

- Do not concern yourself unduly with getting every little detail right, so long as the essential aspects of the plan are rigorously followed through.

- Be prepared to take drastic measures to achieve this, including the removal of dissenters. But try to avoid more than one reorganisation. If some measures are negative, for instance a closedown of some activity or operation, try also to hold out some positive features in the future.

- Be prepared for things turning out less positively than anticipated. But where things go wrong, 'find a shoulder to cry on outside the company'. Providing that shoulder is one of the roles of the interim management company. At EIM, for instance, every interim manager has a permanent staff counsellor he can turn to for advice.

- Do not try to do too much on your own. Working hours will inevitably be long but they should not be unreasonable.

- Bear in mind that somone will usually be taking over from you permanently. Transfer your knowledge to bring about lasting improvements.

PERSONAL OBJECTIVES

In the previous chapter we talked about the difficulty of reconciling the express or implied interests of the various parties in an interim management situation. To that list one should add personal interests. They are embedded in the advice not to work unreasonable hours, and that can be a difficult line to maintain. As EIM's Michael Kelly points out, clients are apt to demand the 'last drop of blood' for their money from interim managers, though working them to exhaustion is no more sensible than doing this to one's permanent staff.

That apart, there are also assignments which should at least be examined very carefully before committing oneself to them. Philip Butler, another EIM interim manager, has some good suggestions. Prior to joining EIM's pool of managers he turned work down for the following reasons:

- Having made his own assessment of the situation, he decided the company was beyond repair.[3]

- The terms of reference within which he would be operating were not clear.

- The level at which he would be operating was too low.

- The assignment did not fit into his personal or marketing strategy — it did not lead anywhere in terms of future assignments he might want to aim for.

The lesson of all this is that one's career does not stop as an interim manager. It merely moves in a different direction, but it takes the same amount of planning as a mainstream career does, or at any rate it should do.

CHECKLIST: HOW AN INTERIM MANAGEMENT FIRM SHOULD SATISFY THE PROSPECTIVE INTERIM MANAGER

It is clear that the range of companies offering interim management services is considerable. There can be significant differences between companies, not only in their size and track record, but in the fundamental ways in which they operate. At the top of the market, firms provide ongoing consultancy through assignments and act as contractual principals with the client. Services range downwards from here to one-man operators acting solely as contact generators. It is important to be clear about the type of organisation being engaged, as a client, or joined, as an interim manager. Basic guidelines should include:

- A prompt and courteous reply to the initial approach by the individual

- A sound marketing strategy, including a sizeable promotional budget

- Good and ongoing contacts with potential clients at a relevant level and, in the case of specialists, in relevant functions

- A sound reputation based on being able to show a good client list and a wide range of successfuly completed assignments

- High quality and properly organised support to interim managers, both on assignment and while on its database

- Satisfactory payment arrangements — notably that settlement should not depend on whether or not the client has paid the interim management intermediary

- Readiness to accept some or all the credit risk, where this may be involved, for instance in turnarounds. P–E International admits that it lost a lot of money in the eventual failure of Lowndes Queensway, a struggling retail group into which it had put a number of interims

- The position regarding legal liability: As well as the risk of not being paid, interim managers appointed as 'shadow directors' in crisis management situations could actually find themselves personally liable if a company was trading illegally (eg while insolvent) – a problem which may not be evident at first. They should check that the interim manager provider has made the fullest possible investigation of its client's true circumstances and, ideally, that it has taken out insurance to indemnify the interim against legal action that may arise in such circumstances. This is also something that interims ought to cover in their own professional indemnity insurance.

- Good client negotiating skills on remuneration, a period of notice and time off for self-marketing, particularly towards the end of the assignment

- The existence on the database of other interim managers comparable to yourself, who are happy with the arrangements and are getting an adequate flow of work through it

- A reasonable mark-up factor in charges to clients.

- No entry fees charged to the interim manager for being included on the databank

- The absence of, or at any rate openness about, other vested interests — some so-called interim management firms also act as a vehicle to sell insurance or financial management to independent consultants.

EXECUTIVE SUMMARY

For an independent consultant, the advantages of working through an intermediary justify the commissions they charge against his or her fee. The interim manager is on the databank of the intermediary, and benefits from their marketing expertise while being able to concentrate on the task in hand.

The best intermediaries also undertake ongoing client/interim manager guidance, if necessary; fee negotiation; securing payment and organising meetings with other interim managers.

Interim management involves the same amount of personal planning as a mainstream career, and some assignments should be examined carefully before commitment is made.

There a number of factors which a prospective interim manager should examine when considering working through an interim management/executive leasing firm, such as its marketing strategy, the extent of its organised support, reasonable charges and payment arrangements, and whether the fee it proposes to clients, and the percentage it takes from the interim manager, are reasonable.

REFERENCES

1. The Independent Consultancy Market, 1991 Annual Survey, GMS, Dunstable.

2. EIM Assignment, Issue no. 1.

3. That point is underlined by Sir Ian McGregor, whose role as chief executive of British Steel and then the National Coal Board was essentially one of interim management. Speaking on the subject on an in-flight tape for British Airways, he listed 'achievable objectives' as important criteria both from a corporate and an individual point of view.

7

Effecting The Introduction: Client Company and Interim Manager

Whatever the differences in preliminary procedures and practices between interim management providers may be, one point on which both they and interim managers themselves are in agreement is the importance of the induction process. Sir Ian McGregor, whose experience as *de facto* interim CEO at British Steel and the National Coal board is unrivalled, sees top level commitment to the assignment as crucial to its success and for this reason interim management firms recommend that the person appointed should be introduced by the chief executive or chairman of the company to the people he will be working with, and in the case of a smaller firm, to the entire staff. That introduction should set out the reporting responsibilities and the tasks of the interim manager, why the appointment has been made and what the interim's credentials are.

There are some spoken and unspoken questions which have been found to predominate in the minds of the permanent staff when an interim appointment has been made, and which the CEO should be prepared to deal with.[1]

> To signal the organisation's commitment to the appointment, the interim manager should be introduced to its key people by the CEO or chairman.

- *Why has it not been made from within?* The answer depends on the situation. Where the interim manager is stepping into a gap, it is usually because no one else can be spared from their ongoing duties. In the case of crisis or turnaround management, it is that a fresh, impartial and experienced eye is needed. See also Chapters 3 and 5 for further details on the reasons for appointing an interim.[2]

- *Is the interim manager a threat to the jobs of those alongside whom he will be working?* The answer is that because of his interim status that is precisely what he will *not* be. Interim managers come, see, conquer, transfer their knowledge — and move on. However, the answer has to be carefully phrased. While the interim manager personally will not be a threat to a specific jobholder, his appointment may well result in recommendations regarding the overall head count or the phasing out of certain activities.

- *Why is the interim manager being paid so much more than equivalent permanent members of staff?* This question will not, of course, surface in the very early stages of an assignment, but managers who think salaries can be kept a secret delude themselves, unless their accounts department is full of unusually discreet people. The answers are set out in the section on 'Comparing The Real Costs' in Chapter 5.

- *If the interim manager is such a 'hot shot' (remembering that as rule he will be over-qualified), why is he doing this?* The person effecting the introduction will have to explain something of the rationale of interim management set out in Chapters 2, 3 and 5.

Interim managers should also 'say a few words', in the view of EIM's Merlin Alty. In fact communication skills are an extremely important attribute for interim managers. But they should not say too much at this point — merely that they have been given an outline of the company and the tasks that are in front of them, who they will be working with in the first instance and that they will be spending the first few days getting acquainted with everybody.

THE FIRST FEW DAYS

A good, concise summary of the important initial stages of an assignment was given by Barry Cramp, an interim executive who specialises in corporate rescues, in an interview published in *The Times*[3]:

> Before he arrives at a business, he studies accounts for the past two years and management accounts for the past six months. For the first few days he talks to management at all levels, assessing their calibre and whether they are in the right job. At the end of the first week, he knows how many people must go, a week later he knows who they are, and by the end of the third week they have gone.

This may sound like drastic action, but in crisis situation that is usually what is required, though Merlin Alty says that he has found that employees of companies in trouble are generally aware of this. He further elaborates on this theme by talking of the need to identify urgent tasks in the first few days of an assignment, but also of the need to reassure frightened people.

> **In crisis management drastic action is often needed. If so, it should be taken with as little delay as possible, and preferably at one blow rather in the form of 'death by a thousand cuts'.**

Here one can take as a text a passage from Machiavelli's classic, *The Prince*,[4] political handbook for 15th century rulers of Italian city states, the relevance of which to present day management was first spotted by Sir Antony Jay (of 'Yes, Minister' fame) in his book *Management and Machiavelli*.[5] Machiavelli wrote:

> It should be noted that when he first seizes a state the new ruler should determine all the injuries he needs to inflict. He should inflict them once and for all, and not have to renew them every day, and in that way he will be able to set men's minds at rest and win them over to him when he confers benefits. Whoever acts otherwise, either through timidity or bad advice, is always forced to have the knife ready in his hand and can never depend on his subjects because they, suffering fresh and continuous violence, can never feel secure with regard to him.

Bringing this advice more mundanely up to date, interim managers should at the same time be aware of the legal limit to their powers regarding dismissal, a point on which employers are often unaware or misinformed. There are elaborate legal provisions in the UK governing wrongful, unfair or constructive dismissal and these are even stricter in other European Community countries.

In fact, at every point of an assignment there is a need to 'engage brain before mouth' in the words of one interim manager. One reason for this is that the job specification is nearly always different from the reality. As was pointed out earlier, problems and their causes often turn out to be different from and sometimes worse than those which have originally been outlined. That is why in spite of the thoroughness of its assignment descriptions, EIM recommends that the specification of what needs doing should not be written in tablets of stone — though at the same time variations should only be introduced with the agreement of the parties concerned. 'We know that in a "crisis" assignment, the situation will nearly always be twice as bad as anyone admits and the amount of help available, half.'

INTERIM MANAGERS AND THE UNOFFICIAL HIERARCHY

Despite what the organisation chart may show, an interim manager must identify the *unofficial* hierarchy. An article in *The Times* on this subject in 1990 made the point that finding one's way around an organisation using the organisation chart as a guide was rather like trying to get around the streets of London with an underground map.

The importance of the unofficial hierarchy, even at top level, has been confirmed by Sir John Harvey-Jones, a rare example in the UK of a top manager turned management guru. Talking of the importance of what he called 'the informal organisation' in his book *Making It Happen* he wrote:

> Unless you have worked out how things actually happen, you have no chance of achieving anything at all.[6]

An important part of the early stages of any assignment is to find out what the structure of the unofficial hierarchy is. One of the advantages of the policy of interim management providers of choosing more mature managers for this role is that they have the experience and the instinct to tap into the reality of organisations, with their subtle networks of gate-keepers, influencers and power brokers: the people who can facilitate things happening or stop them in their tracks. It generally takes permanent newcomers time to come to grips with this aspect of organisations, but as we stated in Chapter 5, people tend to be more open with interims who by the nature of their appointment, stand outside office politics.

CHECKING PROGRESS

In order to maintain the delicate balance of interests that are involved in an interim management situation, the interim management company will check back regularly with the people involved. This may take the form of a regular 'phone call to make sure that everything is progressing according to plan, or may be more formalised as periodic written reports from the interim manager or both in the case of EIM. These are normally followed up, in either case, by meetings with the client organisation to review progress and sort out any problems that have arisen. Typically they are concerned with a need to agree variations in the brief as a result of fresh circumstances coming to light, or sorting out difficulties between the interim manager and some member of the permanent staff.

Whether formal or informal, regular checks that the assignment is going according to plan for all concerned are an important aspect of interim management procedures.

EIM leans towards formal arrangements, based on a clear definition of the assignment at the outset. It cites as key factors against which subsequent progress should be tracked and measured:

- a clearly articulated problem;

- a detailed statement of the task, the expected outcomes, the time in which they are to be achieved and the criteria by which they are to be judged;

- the nature and regularity of controls from the top;

- where the interim manager fits into the organisation;
- the length of the job and the duration of notice.

It is in the light of these considerations that the EIM executive who acts as counsellor to the interim manager rings him up regularly to get a report on progress. That is followed up by a monthly written report covering progress against broad aims and actual against forecast results where these can be quantified. In addition to that EIM meets with the client every three to four weeks to make doubly sure that everything is going according to plan. EIM believes that an important part of the counsellor's function is to maintain the independence of the interim manager throughout the assignment. 'There can be a temptation to "go native" after a period', says Robert Mark of EIM. The element of independence is one of the most powerful tools an interim manager has to effect real changes in an organisation.

Interim management firms also encourage a social side to relationships among the people on its database. This is mainly a benefit to individuals rather than clients but the latter also gain from the existence of formal and informal networks among interim managers. It means that when a problem comes up which the interim manager may not himself have the experience to tackle, he will generally know of a colleague with expert knowledge who does.

PAY PROCEDURES

One of the attractions of interim management, both for clients and the interim managers themselves, is the simplicity of payment procedures. There are, as stated earlier, no extras to take into account. A variation of practice between companies is whether or not an upfront fee is payable. There is usually no charge for an initial consultation, but EIM, for instance, does make a charge once it has been retained to produce an assignment report because that is clearly a consultancy operation. Stream Resources, to quote another example, charges an initial fee once it is asked to make a search for an interim manager and this is refunded when the person is appointed by the client. Other firms use the opposite procedure. They make no charge for the initial consultation, but they do invoice the client for it if they get the assignment.

Apart from that, practice is similar throughout the sector. Clients are invoiced either weekly, fortnightly or monthly and the interim manager is, or should be, paid monthly by return, irrespective of whether or not the client has paid his bill. That risk is assumed by the interim management company.

TERMINATION

One of the questions clients ask interim management companies is: what happens when an assignment comes to an end? Like payment, it is very simple. There are no long drawn-out termination agreements, no legal penalties, no administrative complications. The interim manager simply leaves. There are cases, though these are unusual, where he is offered and accepts a permanent post with the organisation. In such instances, the interim management firm will charge a negotiable fee which equates to a common search fee.

The fact that such offers are unusual is not a sign that organisations that use interim managers are dissatisfied with them. They have more to do with the reluctance of interim managers to go back to regular employment once they have tasted the freedom and variety of working independently and the fact that they are normally too senior for the permanent job. It is, however, quite common for them to continue to be asked to play a part-time or non-executive director role in the companies with whom they have been working. In that case the interim management company generally continues to charge a fee, based on its normal daily rate.

EXECUTIVE SUMMARY

Getting good results from an interim management assignment depends on good preparation and on-going counselling or project management for the assignment.

One of the roles of the interim management company is to draw up a very detailed specification for the assignment, and to match this up with the profile of an individual or, where a shortlist is provided, with a selected group of individuals on the database.

Once the appointment is agreed with the client, commitment must be absolute. The best way of signalling this to people within the organisation is that the appointee is introduced to key people within it by the most senior client sponsor, who should be prepared to answer the key questions staff are likely to raise about such an appointment. The level of spending discretion allowed to the interim is another sign of commitment — or lack of it.

The first few days in an assignment are crucial, especially in a crisis. Drastic action, when needed, should be taken as soon as possible, though the interim must always be aware of its legal, as well as its organisational, implications. The latter may depend very considerably on the structure of the 'unofficial hierarchy' in the organisation. Interim managers are well placed to key into this, by virtue of their experience and the fact that their appointment is no threat to anyone.

At the same time, checking progress with all concerned is vital to the smooth running of an assignment and suitable procedures for doing this are one of the marks of a good interim management firm.

REFERENCES

1. Using Temps Effectively, Reed Employment.

2. Readers interested in how to 'address the troops' in a crisis situation and how to introduce a mission and a train of command should turn to pp. 622–625 of Nigel Hamilton's book on Montgomery, referred to in Chapter 3.

3. Surgeons of Management, 14 February 1991.

4. Machiavelli (1961) *The Prince*, Penguin, London.

5. Kelly, Michael (1991), *Coping With Crisis*, Executive Interim Management, London.

6. Jay, Sir Anthony (1970) *Management and Machiavelli*, Penguin, London.

7. Harvey-Jones, Sir John (1988) *Making It Happen*, Collins, London.

8

Assignment Logistics

The previous chapters have warned against the dangers of interim managers being treated as glorified office temps. In spite of the much greater financial commitment involved in interim management, it can happen. In checking out induction procedures with a number of interim management firms, I came across a firm, one of whose interims had still had not been allotted a desk or a telephone extension after over a week on assignment. Such experiences are rare, but as with any other temporary worker, clients need to make some basic preparations — psychological as well as physical — for the arrival of an interim manager.

Let us begin by looking briefly at the advice given to companies in the Reed Executive booklet referred to in an earlier chapter,[1] because there are some underlying similarities in the principles of what one might call good housekeeping. Under the heading 'Where The Office Ropes Are' it recommends making sure that the geography and security aspects of the building are run through; all support services made available and understood; and house styles and protocols explained.

More significant at the level of managers entering a company is to:

- communicate clearly to the interim manager's direct reports, and other key relationships, the terms of reference of the assignment. If possible, emphasise that the role is an interim one and that the manager is a specialist in this sort of situation;

- effect the right introductions within the company on day one. It can make the learning curve much smoother if a thorough brief is given of key personalities and 'territorial' issues;

- with almost equal urgency, the manager is likely to need introductions to key people with whom the company deals externally. These could range from key suppliers and customers to bankers or institutional shareholders;

- decide and communicate lines of authority within the company. These can be for those people who will work for the new manager, as well as for the reporting structure for the manager himself.

PRELIMINARIES

At the level of interim managers this procedure is inevitably much more sophisticated and elaborate. At EIM, defining the job specification, and everything it will entail, is a highly intensive consultative process for which a charge is made to the client. It should cover the following points:

- **The name of the client** through whom the enquiry has come and the name and function of the person on-site at the assignment to whom the interim manager will be principally responsible.

- **Key details of the organisation or company** where the interim management position is occurring. These include:

[110]

- size by sales volume, number of employees, and number of plants or locations;
- client position in the industry;
- client position in its market sector;
- position of the client organisation in the corporate structure (eg is it a subsidiary and if so, what are its concerns and size in relation to the whole?);
- locations in which active;
- how long established;
- corporate structure.

- **Key issues** include a brief description of the circumstances in which the appointment is being made and the current state of the business.

- **Reasons** why an interim appointee is being proposed, what his key tasks are broadly likely to be and how his appointment will be described.

- **Location and expected duration of the job**, in terms of time and/or number of days work per week.

- **Key working relationships** both in terms of who he will be reporting to and of who will be reporting to him.

- **Specification of more precise tasks, duties and responsibilities** with some indication of objectives and priorities.

> **A systematic job specification, based on a consideration of all the issues that may arise in connection with an interim appointment is vital if an organisation is to make best use of an interim manager.**

The job specification is developed by EIM and agreed with the client. Derek Wallington of Ernst & Young reports that clients sometimes do not have a very clear idea of what is required. In that case he writes the specification and faxes it to the client for comment and amplification. Probably a similar situation often arises when a search and selection firm is retained, but the crucial difference between finding a permanent manager to fit the job description and bringing on an interim is that of speed. Firms with a crisis on their hands do not have the time to undertake a recruitment process or a search, either of which will take anything from two to six months. Interim management/executive leasing providers generally reckon to have a man in position within 7 to 14 days of getting an assignment, though some report occasions when it has been even quicker. To some extent it also depends on whether the client is in a position to make quick decisions on an appointment. For instance, it is obviously quicker to accept the interim provider's nominee than to insist on a shortlist. But interim management firms also stress that the client must be happy with the procedures by which the person is appointed, because it is a key tenet of the whole concept that he then becomes part of the client's team.

Conversely, says Derek Wallington of Ernst & Young, the client must also be committed to the interim manager, a view that is shared by EIM and other interim management firms. EIM's Robert Mark summarises the issues neatly in an article in *Modern Management*:

> Following a detailed brief from the client company, a clearly fomulated definition of the problem and a precise written description of the interim manager's tasks are produced. This describes his or her duties, authority and reporting lines, thus enabling effectiveness to be monitored during the assignment. An agreement will be reached with the client on the time scale, fee rates, monitoring process and the expected duration of the assignment.

The interim manager most suited to the assignment in terms of skills and personal chemistry is selected by the consultancy not the client company,* thus freeing the latter from all the

---

* Note that practice in this regard varies. Some interim management/executive leasing firms do produce a shortlist of candidates for their client to choose from.

ramifications normally associated with taking on new staff. The individual selected will be highly skilled, mature and with broad experience. The necessary experience and qualifications will already have been discussed with the client prior to the appointment to ensure that the right person is picked for the job.

THE CONTRACT AND ITS IMPLICATIONS

Once the assignment specification and person profile has been agreed by the client, this is then followed up by an exchange of contracts between the interim management company and the client; and between the former and the interim manager himself. Note that normally there is no contract between the interim manager and the client for whom he will be working.

Another point, stressed by EIM, is that the contract both with the client and the interim manager is 'for services', not 'of service'. In other words he is working for the client, but he is not of the client's organisation. In the UK this has important tax implications, which should be borne in mind by interim managers. The point is that the Inland Revenue will automatically take the view that anyone on a contract 'of service' is employed by the other party to the contract and will therefore be taxed on the much less advantageous Schedule E (PAYE) basis, rather than as a self-employed Schedule D person.

How the Inland Revenue distinguishes between employed and self-employed people is set out in a leaflet, IR 56, *Employed or Self-Employed*, available from your tax inspector, but even within the wording set out in that, tax inspectors are given considerable leeway regarding its interpretation. Interim management firms therefore advise (and some insist) that interim managers should form themselves into limited companies. These do not run the risk of falling into the tax net in the same way as individuals, and also limit the legal liability of their shareholders; but they do require more administration than simply acting as a sole trader. An accountant or solicitor will be able to explain the details of what is involved.

[113]

EXECUTIVE SUMMARY

To get the best out of an interim manager the company using his services should be expected to effect basic 'good housekeeping' principles, and provide job specifications taking into consideration all the issues which may arise: for instance reporting relationships, house styles, etc.

Appointment procedures vary, depending on time factors, but interim management/executive leasing providers can generally have someone in position within 14 days.

Contracts are exchanged between the client and the provider, and between the provider and the interim manager. The latter is self-employed, and the words of the contract reflect this. An Inland Revenue leaflet, IR56, is available which outlines the definition of self-employment for tax purposes.

REFERENCES

1. Godfrey Golzen, *Using Temps Effectively*, Reed Employment 1988.

9

International Prospects
for Interim Management

Good business ideas spread quickly, so one test of the viability of the concept of interim management is the degree to which it is gaining ground in other countries. The indications are that in a number of economies there is a movement towards organisational flexibility on the one hand, and on the other, increasing interest by mature managers in developing their careers towards greater autonomy. That combination is creating conditions for rapid growth in the market for interim managers, notably in continental Europe and the USA. There are few organisations in the field however, which are organised internationally.

The other factor which is leading to increased use of interim solutions is management of international business. The problems and complexities of running companies at a distance, either in terms of time or kilometres, are all too familiar to most busy executives. There may be problems of distance and communication in one's own country but more often than not the major difficulties arise with an overseas operation, with all its inherent differences in language, culture, mentality and management style; the social, fiscal and legal aspects; and completely different accounting systems and reporting procedures. Even within Europe, in spite of continuing efforts to normalise some, or indeed all of these, differences continue to make it difficult for the executive responsible to keep a preventative finger on the pulse of even a going concern. But more than that, management at a distance has its consequences in the continuity and development of businesses.

The international executive is continually concerned with keeping the business on course in a changing business environment. For example, are the chosen strategic options still valid, has the business climate for a subsidiary changed, should the plans change? Then there are the human resource aspects, selection and recruitment. Are the right people being attracted?

Perhaps most important of all, do the reporting systems reflect what you need to know to monitor the business as well as what local management needs to know to run the business?

Most of the things which go wrong are, in the end, attributed to poor management but often the root of the problem lies in incorrect responses due to lack of, or wrong, information and poor communication. Executives responsible for the international affairs of their companies know that few things go right all of the time. It's not about having doubts or wavering confidence. It is simply about having the resources to manage problems which develop remote from where you are when they are identified.

For example, among EIM's international clients the following are typical of the problems encountered:

- deviation from the strategic path due to emphasis on local firefighting or head office demands;

- market penetration low due to an incorrectly diagnosed approach, inappropriate packaging of the product and lack of attention to local requirements;

- personnel problems due to inappropriate employment contracts and conditons;

- lack of motivation and dynamism due to absence of involvement and commitment, ie things got left to head office;

- sudden departure of key personnel, no captain on the bridge.

All invariably result in falling revenue, rising costs, falling client base, late deliveries, inadequate and incorrect management information, conflicts and loss of profit.

Yet with sights set on 1992 many companies are having to invest in overseas operations. Not all have considered whether they can manage them properly. In the case of acquisitions and mergers of going concerns in particular, there are always areas of additional sensitivity where managing the required change process, and adapting to different cultures are of paramount importance. Quite simply, in many cases, is what you've got really what you thought you'd bought?

The responsibility for performance of a subsidiary company lies jointly with the executive responsible for international operations and the local manager. But if things do go wrong it does not follow that one or both are directly to blame. EIM, for example, has a long, successful track record of carrying out international assignments on behalf of headquarter companies. More than half their assignments are for management at a distance. The use of such services in the country where the problem company is located ensures total familiarity with local legal, fiscal, technical and other requirements. Understanding of the language, culture and local mentality is critical.

Interim management can:

- take over the total management of a company on a temporary basis;

- put stability back into an ailing team;

[117]

- help determine the real priorities, translate them into actions and implement them;
- offer additional skills and experience to an existing organisation;
- improve communications with the headquarters company;
- motivate and stimulate the local work force.

Three territories — the Benelux countries, Germany and the United States — serve to illustrate the past and future potential of interim management internationally.

THE BENELUX COUNTRIES

The strongest manifestation of European interim management to date is in the Benelux countries. EIM's operation in Holland, BCG, has been in existence for 13 years. The management at EIM point to two main reasons for the strength of the concept in the Benelux countries:

1. The prevalence of small and medium-sized family-owned companies. These are often characterised by succession problems of various kinds, for instance, G J Doeksen, one of BCG's interims and a former managing director of a food company, stepped into the breach to guide the Dutch family company which runs the ferry operation to one of the Friesian Islands, a community of 11,000 people. This is a sensitive post, a combination of public service and commercial activity.
    The manager originally designated to tide the company over until junior members of the family could take the helm proved to be unable to manage this relationship and it was necessary to bring in an interim, who by the nature of that kind of appointment, would be able to take a view uncluttered by precedents and also to act

as mentor to the family member designated for eventual succession. Not only is the appointment of an interim the ideal appointment in such situations — they also do not greatly attract good full-time managers in the process of building their careers.

2. Labour laws in this sector of the European Community (and also in Germany) make it extremely difficult to get rid of employees, at any level, for reasons other than misconduct. This obviously makes interim solutions more attractive.

    In the longer term, if employment protection provisions are extended by the Social Charter, it would also greatly increase the demand for interims in other Community countries, notably the UK.

Transferring the power

Ir (engineer) Willem Stoorvogel is the BCG interim manager at GEB, the privatised electricity, gas, waste burning and municipal hot water supply utility for The Hague and its satellite municipality, Voorburg. He manages a staff of 1200 people, and a customer base of 230,000 and is also training his successor, Henk van Eerten. At the same time, he is sorting out a number of problems in the second echelon of management, not least of which is the career shock of finding themselves in a different sort of organisation from the one they originally joined.

His change management brief is to manage the process of turning GEB into a private company, earning profits for its shareholders who include its previous owners. These continue to exert a good deal of influence. For instance, says Stoorvegel, for conservation reasons he has the unusual task of discouraging, rather than stimulating, energy consumption. At the same time he is constrained as to the extent to which he can raise prices.

It is easy to see how such a task would hardly tempt a permanent manager, but Willem Stoorvogel says he is fascinated by the challenge and has the experience to handle it.

GERMANY

EIM has people working in Italy, France and Spain. The biggest immediate potential, however, is in Germany.

EIM has offices in Munich, Frankfurt and Berlin already showing signs of rapid expansion, under the direction of Norbert Eisenberg. Germany, he says, already has a base of several hundred independent consultants working through banks and on an *ad hoc* basis with established 'big name' consultancy firms. But despite high fee levels, running at around £1000 a day, independents in Germany do not as yet have the prestige which attaches there to being a full-time employee in a top job. Eisenberg thinks that working through interim management intermediaries could bridge that status gap. There is also growing acceptance, especially in capital goods producing companies, that appointing interim managers in change and crisis situations makes sound commercial sense.

Probably the biggest source of work will be East Germany. There are literally thousands of formerly state-owned industrial and commercial units there which are crying out for managers who can apply and transfer western experience and know-how. However, not many successful managers from the west want to go and live in the east, where conditions are still comparatively primitive.

Eisenberg believes that the demand for interims, mainly in East Germany, could have reached 2000 by the end of the decade, with an annual fee value running into several hundred million Deutschmarks.

Inevitably this prospect is attracting competitors, in addition to the already established supplier of interim managers,

AC Alpha Consulting AG. The most notable of these is Korn/Ferry/Haselmann Interim Management GmBH, based in Frankfurt. Like Egon Zehnder, co-partners in EIM, Korn/Ferry is an international executive search firm. It has set up a joint interim management venture with Dr Haselmann, the former CEO of Alpha Consulting, who is generally credited with having pioneered interim management in Germany.

He too sees Eastern Europe and particularly East Germany as a major market and his profile of the ideal interim is much the same as that of other players — that is, someone with a good track record, all-round high-level experience for general management positions (or high-level experience for general management positions), who has reached a point where they have gained financial independence, but who still has the edge and toughness to handle change management.

THE UNITED STATES

The biggest growth of all, however, will probably come from the world's biggest economy: the USA. According to a study of the US workforce quoted in a recent newsletter from IMCOR, a leading US supplier of interim managers, most large American employers are scaling down their permanent staff and replacing them with 'contingent workers': temporaries, part-timers and sub-contractors.

Of this expanding sector, interim management is showing the most rapid growth. Some 22 interim management providers have set up in business in the past couple of years in the USA. At the same time, says the report, interim managers are being identified as among 'the best and the brightest': first-rate professionals who do not want to become full-time core employees, but who prefer the challenge of short-term assignments. From an employer's point of view, they have the further advantage of immediate availability.

In a commercial environment in which what Tom Peters calls 'the millisecond advantage' can be crucial and where the concept of 'just in time' resourcing is being extended to people as well as materials, interim management has a bright future ahead of it — wherever in the world you look.

There are valuable lessons in this for UK family companies. A survey of such business, conducted by the accountants Stoy Hayward and the London Business School (published by Kogan Page in 1991 as *The Stoy Hayward Guide To Family Business*) highlights the enormous difficulties encountered by UK family companies in the succession process. Interim managers, acting both as a buffer between the past and future management of such companies, and as mentor to family board members, could play a very useful role here.

EXECUTIVE SUMMARY

The problems of managing international business are leading to increased use of interim management. This is due to a number of factors: the world-wide trend towards organisational flexibility, the aspirations for career autonomy by senior managers and, in some countries, general business conditions or specific legislation which makes temporary solutions attractive.

The latter is particularly true of the Benelux countries, where interim management is strongly established. Consequently, it is able to attract very high calibre interims to tackle what are often extremely challenging management assignments.

Interim management is spreading to a number of countries in Continental Europe. There is great potential in Germany, particularly East Germany, where many industries need western experience and know-how, but cannot attract permanent employees to what is still a comparatively primitive environment.

Among the biggest growth is expected to come from the US, where most employers are scaling down their permanent staff and replacing them with 'contingent' workers. Some 22 interim management providers have set up in business in the US over the past two years.

EIM OFFICES — INTERNATIONAL ADDRESSES

Amsterdam
BCG Interim Management BV
Noordhollandstraat 71
NL-1081 AS Amsterdam
The Netherlands

Tel: (31) 20-6464771/6465591
Fax: (31) 20-6610699/6440245

Berlin
Kurfurstendamm 72
D-1000 Berlin 31
Germany

Tel: (49) 30-323016
Fax: (49) 30-3246298

Brussels
Avenue F Roosevelt 14
B-1050 Brussels
Belgium

Tel: (32) 2-6470171
Fax: (32) 2-6487866

Dusseldorf
Konigsallee 30
D-4000 Dusseldorf
Germany

Tel: (49) 211-13999-0
Fax: (49) 211-13999-31

Frankfurt
Mainzer Landstrasse 46
D-6000 Frankfurt/Main 1
Germany

Tel: (49) 69-7241215
Fax: (49) 69-725014

Hamburg
Ballindamm 5
D-2000 Hamburg 1
Germany

Tel: (49) 40-323240-0
Fax: (49) 40-323240-70

London
Devonshire House
Mayfair Place
London W1X 5FH
United Kingdom

Tel: (44) 71-629 2832
Fax: (44) 71-355 3437

Milan
Piazza Meda 3
I-20121
Milan
Italy
Tel: (39) 2-76020900
Fax: (39) 2-76021063

Munich
Brienner Strasse 43
D-8000 Munich 2
Germany

Tel: (49) 89-593727
Fax: (49) 89-5231867

Paris
12 Avenue George V
F-75008 Paris
France

Tel: (33) 1-44318120
Fax: (33) 1-47203982

Zurich
Toblerstrasse 80
CH-8044 Zurich
Switzerland

Tel: (41) 1-2612702
Fax: (41) 1-2511030

Melbourne
Level 27
333 Collins St
Melbourne
Victoria 3000
Australia

Tel: (61) 3-6297260
Fax: (61) 3-6297269

Sydney
Level 65, MLC Centre
19 Martin Place
Sydney NSW 2000
Australia

Tel: (61) 2-232 3855
Fax: (61) 2-221 6420

Appendix 1

Comparative Table of Interim Management Services

Firm	Founded	Offices	Specialisations	Assignments per annum	Charges per day (£)
Albermarle	1986	1 London	–	n/a	400–550
Barton	1990	1 Plymouth	–	n/a	200–500
EIM	1986	13 Amsterdam Berlin Brussels Dusseldorf Frankfurt Hamburg London Melbourne Milan Munich Paris Sydney Zurich	Director & above all sectors	200	650–1500
Ernst & Young	–	–	–	–	–
Extra	1990	–	Banking	5	300–1500
GMS	1983	3 Bradford Bristol London	–	60	200–500
Intex	?	4 Brussels London Paris Stockholm	–	100	250–400
Institute of Directors	1984	1 London	–	n/a	n/a
PA	1990	14 UK	Board level	100	300–1200
PE-Inbucon	–	–	–	–	–
Praxis	1988	1 Birmingham	Department	30	375–650
Profit Management Group	1990	2	Marketing; Finance; Operations	20	200–750
Protem	1990	–	–	15	–
Triple A	–	–	–	–	–
Varley Walker	1988	3 Birmingham London Newcastle	–	n/a	350–550

Appendix 2

Directory

Albemarle Interim Management Services Ltd
18 Great Marlborough Street
London W1V 1AF

Tel: 071-437 3611   Fax: 071-287 8994

Contacts: John Hird, Chris Behan

Sphere of Operations: Founded in 1986, AIMS operates only in the UK, from its London office. It does not specialise in any particular industry, discipline or level. The number of its assignments over the past 12 months is not available.

Method of Operation: AIMS acts either as a principal or an agent, depending on the circumstances and the client's requirements. Following preliminary consultations — free unless AIMS is retained — it produces a shortlist of two or three interim managers, for whom references are provided to the client, though these are also checked by AIMS. A programme of progress checking and reporting during the course of the assignment is agreed with the client.

Charges: A daily rate of between £400–£550 a day is charged weekly to the client.

Barton Interim Management
Bere Barton, Bere Ferrers
Yelverton
Devon PL20 7JL

Tel: 0822 840220   Fax: 0822 841134
Contact: Nicky Cutts

Sphere of Operations: Founded in 1990, BIM is a sister organisation to Barton Executive Search and Barton Non-Executive Directors. It has one office in Plymouth and does not specialise in any particular sphere. The number of its assignments over the past 12 months is not disclosed on confidentiality grounds but 10 per cent of these were abroad.

Method of Operations: Barton operates as a principal/contractor. Pre-assignment consultancy to define the nature of the task is undertaken and not charged for unless Barton is retained. A short-list of interim managers is then put forward, references being checked either by Barton or the client — or both.

Interims are required to carry their own professional indemnity insurance. In the course of the assignment, frequent contact is maintained — at least weekly — both with the client and the interim manager and BIM regards itself as being responsible for the overall management of the assignment.

Charges: From £200–£500 a day, depending on the nature, duration and location of the assignment. Billing, agreed in advance, is weekly or monthly.

Executive Interim Management
Devonshire House
Mayfair Place
London W1X 5FH

Tel: 071-629 2832   Fax: 071-355 3437

Contacts: Robert Mark, Michael Kelly

Sphere of Operations: Founded 1978. Offices in Amsterdam, Brussels, Paris, Zurich, Munich, Frankfurt, Berlin, Dusseldorf, Hamburg, Milan, Sydney, Melbourne. Associated with Europe's leading executive search company Egon Zehnder and with BCG Interim Management BV in the Netherlands.

EIM's various offices handled 200 assignments in the past year. Sixty of these came through the UK office. Of those, 30 per cent were in continental Europe.

EIM operates both in industry and in the service sector, at senior general management and head of function level: mainly MD or FD. Others include: finance, production, IT and commercial directors.

Methods of Operation: Having checked references, EIM puts forward one name only to the client and acts as a principal, regarding itself as wholly responsible for the assignment. That includes legal responsibility for performance. Preceding the assignment, a job and person specification is developed through a process of consultancy and problem diagnosis. A charge is made for this.

During the course of the assignment, EIM is in regular contact with the interim manager and requires him to keep records and analyses of progress. It also meets every three/four weeks with the client, with and without the presence of the interim manager.

Charges: In the UK, £650–£1000 per day.

The Ernst & Young Temporary Executive Service
Becket House
Lambeth Palace Road
London SE1 7EU

Tel: 071-931 4545   Fax: 071-931 4080

Contact: Derek Wallington

Sphere of Operations: Founded in 1988 as part of the Corporate Resources division within the management consultancy arm of the international accountants, Ernst & Young. It operates out of five offices and carried out 16 assignments over the past year, predominantly in the UK. It operates across all functions, industries and disciplines. However, because of E & Y's accountancy base, financial projects predominate.

Method of Operation: E&Y's Temporary Executive Service acts both as a principal and as an agent, depending on circumstances. It does not undertake pre-assignment consultancy.

On being retained, it puts forward a shortlist of candidates, whose references have been checked by Derek Wallington. Candidates are recommended to carry professional indemnity insurance. In the course of the assignment, progress is checked on average once a month and support is provided to the interim manager if the situation warrants it.

Charges: Daily fees between £350–£550

Extra Management Services Ltd
20 The Causeway
Bishops Stortford
Herts CM23 2EJ

Tel: 0279 755686   Fax: 0279 758456

Contact: Craven Vaughan

Sphere of Operations: EMS was founded in November 1990 and has so far handled five assignments, all in the UK. It specialises in banking arrangements and relationships.

Method of Operation: EMS acts as a principal/contractor and conducts a pre-assignment diagnosis of the situation, for which a fee is charged if it is retained. Usually only one name is put forward to the client and references are then checked in conjunction with him. EMS regards the interims with which it deals as a network of independent consultants and they are responsible for making their own business arrangements with clients. However, during the course of the assignment, there are monthly meetings between EMS and the interim, at which progress is discussed. Interims are expected to carry professional indemnity policies.

Charges: £300–£1500 per day.

GMS Consultancy Ltd
48 High Street North
Dunstable
Bedfordshire LU6 1LA

Tel: 0582 666970   Fax: 0582 471757

Contact: Charles Russam

Sphere of Operations: GMS was founded in 1983 and has two other offices in Bristol and Bradford. It handled approximately 60 assignments in the past year, of which three were abroad. It does not specialise in any particular discipline, function or level.

Method of Operation: GMS operates mainly as an agent and puts forward a shortlist to the client. It will also undertake a pre-assignment diagnostic review of the situation and reference checks, if required by the client. GMS does not, however, accept legal liability for the performance of interim managers, though it encourages them to carry professional indemnity insurance.

During the course of the assignment there is frequent contact and discussion with the interim manager and the client, though GMS regards the client/interim manager relationship as being confidential between those two parties.

Charges: Mostly monthly billings, at an average daily rate between £200–£500.

Interim Financial Executives Ltd
Centre Point
103 New Oxford Street
London WC1A 1QF

Tel: 071-499 1611   Fax: 071-497 3600

Contact: Anthony Jackson

Sphere of Operations: Founded in 1990, the firm specialises in the financial sector. 50 per cent of its assignments are abroad, though it does not disclose the total number handled over the last 12 months.

Method of Operation: IFEL operates as a principal and accepts limited legal liability for the work of its interims. It generally puts forward only one name to the client, having first, if the client requires it, undertaken pre-assignment consultancy. During the course of the job it maintains contact with the client and offers back-up to the interim manager as and when necessary.

Charges: Fees range between £250–£500 per day.

Intex Executive Leasing International Ltd
31 Bedford Square
London WC1B 3SQ

Tel: 071-323 2722   Fax: 0303 262185

Contact: David Searle

Sphere of Operations: Intex was founded in 1973 and has two offices in the UK. It also has associated offices in Stockholm, Paris and Brussels. It has handled approximately 100 assignments in the past 12 months, of which 20 per cent were abroad. It does not specialise in any particular field, function or level.

Method of Operation: Intex puts forward a shortlist of two or three candidates to the client. It is responsible for checking references and also accepts legal liability for interim managers' performance. It gets feedback in the course of the assignment, but being an agent rather than a contractor, Intex does not maintain regular progress checks.

Charges: A daily rate between £250–£400.

The Institute of Directors, Executive Resource
116 Pall Mall
London SW1Y 5ED

Tel: 071-839 1233   Fax: 071-930 1949

Contact: Derek Wilson

Founded 1984.
Sphere of Operations: UK only. Operates at board level, but number of assignments not stated.

Methods of Operation: The IOD charges a search fee to clients and checks references of the interim managers it puts forward. They may supply either a short-list or a single name, depending on the client's requirements. The IOD has no further involvement in the assignment beyond that.

Charges: No figure stated

PA Consulting Group
123 Buckingham Palace Road
London SW1W 9SR

Tel: 071-730 9000   Fax: 071-333 5102

Contact: Martin Wood

Sphere of Operations: The formal executive leasing activities of the PA Consulting Group started in 1990, though the company says it has been putting in interim managers, *de facto*, for a number of years. PA has 14 UK offices and 63 elsewhere in the world. 50 per cent of its executive leasing activity is outside the UK and this is reflected in the spread of the approximately 100 assignments it has handled in the past year. These have been mainly at or just below board level across a wide variety of private and public sector organisations.

Method of Operation: The PA Consulting Group acts as a principal. Having conducted a pre-assignment consultancy exercise, it puts forward up to three short-list names, depending on the type of assignment and the client's preferences.

Professional indemnity is covered by PA, which also checks references. During the course of the assignment the interim manager is required to produce reports and analyses of progress. There is regular consultation with the interim manager and back-up is provided as and when required.

Charges: A daily fee rate of between £300–£1200

The P-E/CBI Temporary Executive Service
Park House
Wick Road
Egham
Surrey TW20 0HW

Tel: 0784 434411   Fax: 0784 437828

Contact: Dr R H Penfold

Sphere of Operations: P-E as a consultancy was established in 1934, but its activities in providing interim managers in conjunction with the CBI date from 1981. It operates from seven UK offices and although the number of assignments in the last 12 months is not available, 10 per cent of these were abroad. Most work is senior functional or general management at director level.

Method of Operation: The P–E/CBI service operates primarily as an agent, though it does undertake a pre-assignment consultancy/diagnostic exercise with the client and is responsible for checking references on the candidates put forward on the short-list. However P–E/CBI does not accept legal liability for the performance of its interims, who are required to work through their own limited companies. During the course of the assignment contact is with the client — not the interim manager — and the CBI maintains close checks on the quality of interims' work. The CBI also conducts regular audits of all clients to check on whether they are satisfied with the service they are getting.

*Charges:*Figures are not disclosed.

Profit Management Group Ltd
PO Box 1802
Boxford
Colchester CO6 5NW

Tel: 0787 211185   Fax: 0787 210379

Contact: David Lynch

Sphere of Operations: PMG was founded in 1990 and operates as a network under a marketing umbrella extending from two offices in the UK. It undertook 20 assignments in the past 12 months, one of which was abroad. It tends to specialise in marketing, finance and operations across a wide range of industries.

Method of Operation: PMG operates both as a principal/ contractor and as an agent. It undertakes a pre-assignment consultancy exercise when required which is sometimes the subject of a charge, depending on the circumstances. It then puts forward a list of three suitable candidates. PMG checks their references, but does not accept legal liability for their performance, nor is professional indemnity insurance a mandatory requirement.
    During the course of the assignment contact with the

interim manager is maintained, at least monthly and usually fortnightly, and regular reports and analyses are required.

Charges: £200–£750 per day

PRAXIS
18 Bennets Hill
Birmingham B2 5QJ

Tel (and Fax) 021 616 2242

Contact: Carl Hague

Founded 1988. One office. A specialist interim management consultancy. It has no other related activities or associated companies.

Sphere of Operations: Praxis handled approximately 30 assignments in the last 12 months, of which 50 per cent were abroad, mainly in continental Europe. It focuses on 'Times Top 1000' companies in all sectors, at head of function/head of department level.

Methods of Operation: Praxis acts as a principal/contractor. It undertakes pre-assignment consultancy with prospective clients, for which there is no charge. Clients are given a choice of up to three interims (Praxis uses the the term, Locums) and references are checked by both parties. Interim managers are required to have professional indemnity insurance, though Praxis also carries it on its own behalf.

During the course of an assignment regular site visits — at least every four weeks — are undertaken to check progress.

Charges: Daily rates of between £375–£650.

APPENDIX 2

Protem
100 Piccadilly
London W1V 9FN

Tel: 071-355 3683   Fax: 071-734 9581

Contact: Richard Ball

Sphere of Operations: Protem was founded in 1991 by the executive search firm Heidrick & Struggles International and has access to its parent company's worldwide network of offices. In the last twelve months, three assignments have been in Continental Europe, out of a total of 15. The accent is on senior functional, project and general and management, mainly in crisis or turnround situations.

Method of Operation: After a preliminary discussion with the client (sometimes followed by a more detailed business audit for which a fee is charged), Protem prepares an 'assignment and person profile'. A search for an interim manager is then conducted through Heidrick & Struggles and other sources, from which a shortlist of two or three is presented to the client. This process, however, takes days rather than the weeks required for full-scale search.

Protem strongly recommends that interims should carry professional indemnity insurance, but otherwise sees the relationship as one between the client and interim manager, in which its own role is limited to 'collegiate discussion'. Richard Ball feels that at the level at which Protem is operating, interim managers rarely need advice from an intermediary, though it is available informally when they do.

Charges: Monthly fees of £10,000–£15,000 are paid to interim managers, after Protem has deducted a management charge of one third. For the client, there is a minimum charge per assignment of £20,000 plus VAT.

Touche Ross Interim Executives
Hill House
1 Little New Street
London EC4A 3TR

Tel: 071-936 3000   Fax: 071-583 4551

Contact: John Brookes

Sphere of Operations: UK, Europe and the Middle East. Board and senior management assignments in both the private and public sectors.

Method of Operation: Touche Ross charges a service fee to clients when an interim executive is appointed from a short list of candidates provided. The executive charges the client direct.

Charges: 20 per cent of fees charged by the interim executive.

Triple A Group Ltd
18 Lawrence Avenue
New Malden
Surrey KT3 5LY

Tel: 081-335 3135   Fax: 081-337 8297

Contact: Derek Mortimer

Triple A states that because of the flexibility required to meet client needs and because of commercial confidentiality, it is unable to provide details of its operations, beyond the fact that its interim managers are 'mature, independent, often multilingual professionals, some of whom live, or have lived in continental Europe'.

Varley Walker Interim Management Ltd
St James House
17 Horsefair
Birmingham B1 1DB

Tel: 021-622 1133   Fax: 021-666 6955

Contact: Alan Horn

Sphere of Operations: Founded in 1988, Varley Walker Interim Management Ltd is part of the recruitment and human resource consultancy, Varley Walker. It has offices in London, Birmingham and Newcastle. The number of assignments over the last 12 months is not available, but 5 per cent of these were abroad. Assignments tend to be either senior managerial or project management jobs across a wide scope of industries and disciplines.

Method of Operation: Varley Walker acts as agent on interim assignments. It will, if required, conduct a pre-assignment consultancy and diagnostic exercise and this is charged for if the company is retained. The number of candidates then put forward depends on the client's requirements.

Interims are required to carry professional indemnity insurance, and reference checking is carried out by Varley Walker. The firm requires regular feedback. It meets with the interim on- or off-site once a month and asks for an end of assignment brief which is discussed with the client.

Charges: £300–£550 per day.

Contract Terms

Guidelines from Executive Interim Management

A. CONTRACT BETWEEN CLIENT AND INTERIM MANAGEMENT PROVIDER

Duties of the interim management provider
These depend on whether the interim management provider is acting as an agent or a principal. EIM, for example, operates as a principal and undertakes to supervise the interim manager. The client is required to provide guidance, facilities, information and assistance to enable the interim to carry out the task. However, neither an agent nor a principal — nor, of course, the interim manager him- or herself — is an employee of the client. They are merely providing a service.

Duration of service
This is generally for a fixed period of time with a provision to extend, with the agreement of both parties.

Remuneration
The daily rate at which the service is charged and the terms

of payment — eg monthly or weekly. Normally payment is to the provider, not to the individual interim manager.

Expenses
Expenses are normally paid direct to the interim manager on a previously agreed basis.

Termination
In the case of EIM, the contract can be terminated with one month's notice, either by the client or EIM. Some interim management providers introduce a variable whereby the arrangement can be terminated at 24 hours notice within, say, the first month of an assignment. After that, a month's notice is required. There may also be a clause allowing for faster termination in exceptional circumstances.

Retention
Interim managers are sometimes asked to stay on as permanent staff. The fee, if any, payable to the provider of the interim manager should this happen, should be specified.

Liability
The question of who is liable for damages if the interim manager fails to perform should be spelled out, as well as the criteria for such an eventuality.

Confidentiality
The secrecy of confidential information given to the provider of interim management must be preserved.

Arbitration
It is often agreed that disputes between the parties be settled through an abitrator chosen in agreement by both of them.

B. CONTRACT BETWEEN THE INTERIM MANAGER AND THE INTERIM MANAGEMENT PROVIDER

Duties of the interim manager
Sets out what the interim manager is required to do and the nature of his reports.

Duration

The contract is set for a fixed period with a provision to extend, subject to agreement.

Remuneration

The basis of payment (usually a daily rate) and how often it is due. Payment is through the interim management provider, but the interim manager in the UK must ensure that this does not lay him open to PAYE assessment by the Inland Revenue. Many providers suggest that interims should form limited companies, payment through whom is treated differently to individual payments.

Expenses

Usually paid direct to the interim by the client, rather than the interim management intermediary. The nature of recoverable expenses should be agreed beforehand by the parties concerned.

Termination

See Contract A.

Liability

The interim manager is under a legal obligation, framed in the Trade Descriptions Act, to carry out the services he is offering to standards satisfactory to the client. Those standards should be agreed beforehand to minimise the possibility of liability litigation, but interims are also advised to carry professional indemnity liability insurance.

Confidentiality

See Contract A.

Competition and constraints

The interim management provider may ask the interimn manager to agree not to work for a client company which is in competition with a previous client for an agreed time — usually not more than 12 months.

Arbitration

See Contract A.

Appendix 4

Professional Indemnity Insurance and The Interim Executive

Professional Indemnity is essential protection for the consultant. It is commercially prudent to hold a Professional Indemnity policy and it is often seen as the hallmark of a professional approach. Some professions by law have to hold a Professional Indemnity policy, eg accountants and solicitors.

The purpose of Professional Indemnity Insurance is to protect the individual during the course of providing his services against legal liability to compensate third parties who have sustained some injury, loss or damage due to professional negligence.

THE ATIES PROFESSIONAL INDEMNITY PLAN

Robert Barrow has designed a Professional Indemnity Insurance Scheme for the Association of Temporary and Interim Executive Services called the ATIES Professional Indemnity Insurance Plan for independent consultants, temporary executives and interim managers (see page 151). The Scheme is underwritten by the Sun Alliance Insurance Company and is designed to cover claims arising out of professional negligence occurring on ATIES assignments and indeed all other project work performed.

- Cover is available for a wide range of professions and the policy will also pay legal fees to defend claims for professional negligence.

- The ATIES Professional Indemnity Plan has an optional Liability section providing, additional cover for Employers, Public and Products Liability.

- By law anyone trading as a limited company has to have Employers Liability Insurance and the ATIES Professional Indemnity Plan provides unlimited cover.

- The Public Liability Extension covers the consultant's legal liability to third parties who have sustained injury, loss or damage.

- The Products Liability Extension covers the consultant's legal liability to third parties arising out of products sold, supplied, manufactured or repaired.

HOW MUCH DOES THIS COST?

The cost depends on the indemnity limit selected, the type of work to be performed, estimated fees and previous claims history.

The minimum limit of indemnity for Professional Indemnity is £50,000 and the interim executive is advised to purchase as much cover as he or she can afford. A Professional Indemnity policy can be regarded as a sleep at night insurance policy.

The minimum premium is £180 and the premiums are very competitive.

THE ATIES PROFESSIONAL INDEMNITY PLAN

Brokers to ATIES
Robert Barrow Limited
24–26 Minories
London
EC3N 1BY

ATIES Professional Indemnity Plan

The ATIES Professional Indemnity Plan is a unique Insurance Scheme designed by Robert Barrow exclusively for Independent Consultants, Temporary Executives and Interim Managers. The Scheme is underwritten by The Sun Alliance Insurance Company.

Once you have been accepted into the plan it will provide cover for all assignments carried out on your own behalf or for an ATIES member.

What is the purpose of the ATIES Professional Indemnity Plan?

The purpose is to protect the interim manager against Legal Liability to compensate third parties who have sustained some injury, loss or damage due to negligence.

What will the ATIES Professional Indemnity Plan cover?

The Plan will cover claims arising out of professional negligence occurring on ATIES' assignments and indeed other project work that you may perform.

Cover is available for a wide range of professions.

The ATIES Professional Indemnity Plan will also pay legal fees to defend claims for professional negligence.

The ATIES Professional Indemnity Plan also has an optional Liability section providing additional cover for Employers, Public and Products Liability.

How much does this cost?

The cost will depend on the indemnity limit selected, type of work to be performed, estimated fees and previous claims history.

By selecting the ATIES Plan you will benefit from the special discount arranged by ATIES. The minimum premium is £180.

How do I obtain a quotation?

Complete the proposal form and send back to Hilary Wilkins or Steven Barnett at

[152]

Robert Barrow Limited
24–26 Minories
London
EC3N 1BY

Telephone: 071-709 9611
Facsimile: 071-481 4361
Telex: 885576 BARROW G

ATIES PROFESSIONAL INDEMNITY PLAN

A Professional Indemnity policy designed exclusively for Independent Consultants, Temporary Executives and Interim Managers arranged by The Association of Temporary and Interim Executive Services (ATIES).

Proposal Form

1. a) Name and Address: Phone Number:

_____

2. Full description of Proposer's Business:

_____

3. Date of commencement of Business (*Partnership, Sole Trader, Limited Company*):

_____

4. Number of branches from which you operate:

_____

5. a) Estimated Gross Fees for coming 12 months   £   £

   b) Estimated wage roll for the forthcoming
      period   £   £

_____

6. a) Has any claim such as would be covered by the proposed insurance ever been made against this Firm or any of its Partners/Principals whilst in this or any other Business?
                                                        YES/NO

   If yes, full details must be given:

[154]

b) Has the Business been involved in any disputes or arbitrations concerning fees or services to others or any other matters?   YES/NO

If yes, full details must be given:

c) Have you become aware during the last 5 years of any injury to or death, disease or illness arising out of your business of

i) Employees?
ii) Members of the public or damage to their property?

d) Have you been prosecuted during the last 5 years under any safety legislation?   YES/NO

---

7. Are any of the Partners/Directors/Principals or employees, AFTER ENQUIRY, aware of or suspect or have any ground for suspecting any circumstances which might give rise to a claim against the Business or against any of the present of former Partners/Principals?   YES/NO

---

8. Has the Business previously been insured for Professional Indemnity or Employers/Public/Products Liability?
                                                                 YES/NO

If yes, please give:

a) Name of Insurers

b) Indemnity Limit

c) Date of expiry of cover

---

9. Has any Insurer ever:

   a) Declined a proposal or renewal for this Business or any
      Partner/Principal?   YES/NO

      If yes, please provide details:

   _____

10. Do you require cover for Employers Liability and Public and
    Products Liability (unlimited Indemnity in respect of Employ-
    ers Liability and £1M for Public/Products Liability)?
                                                         YES/NO

   _____

11. I/We declare that the statements and particulars in this
    proposal are true and that I/We have not mis-stated or
    supressed any material facts. I/We agreed that this proposal,
    together with any other information supplied by me/us shall
    form the basis of any contract of insurance effected thereon. I/
    We undertake to inform the Insurers of any material alteration
    to these facts whether occurring before or after completion of
    the Contract of Insurance.

    Dated this   day of   19

    Signature of Partner or Director:

    If Business produces a brochure please attach.

**Please return completed Proposal Form to Hilary Wilkins or Steven
Barnett at Robert Barrow Limited.**

Index

INDEX